Truly Called?

Vocation in the Anglican Church

Bradly Billings

Truly Called? Vocation in the Anglican Church
Bradly Billings

First published in 2023
by Broughton Publishing Pty Ltd
32 Glenvale Crescent Mulgrave VIC 3170

Copyright © Bradly Billings 2023

All rights reserved. No part of this publication may be reproduced, stored in a retrieval system or transmitted, in any form or by any means electronic, photocopying, recording or otherwise, without the prior written permission of the publisher.

Cover Design: WorkingType Studio

ISBN 978-1-9224410-7-2

Contents

Foreword	iv
Dedication	viii
Introduction	ix
Terminology	xiii
Abbreviations	xiv

PART A – VOCATION AND CALLING

1. Being – know yourself	2
2. When God speaks your name	15
3. Qualities and characteristics	29
4. Becoming – formation for ministry	49

PART B – THE ANGLICAN WAY

5. Anglican ordination	63
6. A unique history – Anglicans in Australia	85
7. Anglican belief and practice	100
Postscript – the testing of vocation	122
Appendix 1	132
Appendix 2	134
Appendix 3	135
Appendix 4	137
Appendix 5	152
Appendix 6	159
Appendix 7	164
Appendix 8	169
Selected Resources	175

Foreword

By The Right Revd Denise Ferguson, The Most Revd Dr Philip Freier, The Right Revd Dr Murray Harvey, The Revd Gary O'Brien and The Revd Dr Raewynne J Whiteley

The Right Revd Denise Ferguson

Discerning a call to ordained ministry is much greater than marking skills or abilities on a matrix. It is the recognition of an ontological call of and by God that sits at the core of ones being. It is a highly complex, private and public journey, that must be examined and affirmed by the wider Church. It is a lifelong journey of formation, being shaped and moulded to grow into the person God has created.

In this book, *Truly Called? Vocation in the Anglican Church* Brad explores the complexities of call and vocation for ordained leadership in the Anglican Church of Australia for both the enquirer, and those who might be privileged to accompany a person on this journey.

Brad specifically addresses an often overlooked, but essential aspect of this discipline. Knowledge of God, and deep, honest knowledge of self, or of one's own personhood. When we truly love God then we can begin the interior journey of exploration of self, a journey that helps us to understand and recognise our calling, which may or may not lead to ordained leadership. However, it will lead to the revelation of which part of the divine dance of discipleship a person has been called to embrace.

The Right Revd Denise Ferguson is Assistant Bishop of the Diocese of Adelaide and Chair St Barnabas College Council.

* * *

THE MOST REVD DR PHILIP FREIER

It has been a great joy to ordain many men and women during the course of my ministry as a Bishop in God's church. Over the past several years I have worked closely in this area with Bishop Brad Billings, who has overseen a program of discernment and selection in this diocese for those who have sensed a calling to the ordained ministry.

This helpful volume arises out of Bishop Brad's extensive experience in this area. It is written for those who believe they may be experiencing a call to ordained ministry in the context of the Anglican Church of Australia. What has been produced is a much needed resource that can be placed into the hands of those contemplating the call of God on their lives, to both inform and educate, and to foster careful and prayerful reflection on these important matters.

I commend this new book as a valuable and timely gift to our Church, as we seek to encourage and nurture the next generation of ordained leaders.

The Most Revd Dr Philip Freier is the Archbishop of Melbourne.

* * *

THE RIGHT REVD DR MURRAY HARVEY

There has been a need for a book like this in the Anglican Church of Australia for a long time. For those sensing a call to the ordained ministry and for those accompanying them, starting out on a journey of discernment can be a daunting task. Those of us who have journeyed with people exploring their call and vocation have, until now, been guided by excellent resources from the Church of England and other places. From his experience and wisdom on this topic Bradly Billings now offers this book to the Australian church. Billings has a deep knowledge and understanding of call and vocation to the ordained ministry, developed from his considerable experience of working in this field as a priest and more recently as a bishop.

As the author rightly reminds us, vocational discernment is not only the work of the person who senses a call to ordained ministry, it is also the church's work – in fact one of the most important tasks of the church. He sees this task as fundamentally missional in nature, as well as being grounded in, and responsive to, the ordinal. Through careful attention to discernment, selection and formation, the church is raising up gifted leaders for tomorrow's church.

The book will be helpful both to those who are exploring a call and to those in the church who are responsible for selection and discernment. While focused on the Australian Anglican context, the key elements and questions identified by Billings for this journey of vocational discernment will also be useful to a wider audience.

The Right Revd Dr Murray Harvey is the Bishop of Grafton NSW.

* * *

THE REVD GARY O'BRIEN

We find ourselves, as Christians today, in a society that is moving rapidly away from its connections with the church. Increasingly, we are on the margins in public discourse. Yet, the gospel message of Jesus needs to be shared and lived, for it is still the "good news", our only hope. To help us in our mission in the world we need leaders, men and women of sound gospel convictions, godly character and solid competencies.

In *Truly called? Vocation in the Anglican Church*, Brad focuses attention on the high calling that ordained ministry is, especially in an Anglican context, and provides assistance and support for men and women under God in thinking through whether this leadership is right for them.

The Revd Gary O'Brien is the Director, Ministry Training & Development of the Anglican Diocese of Sydney.

*   *   *

The Revd Dr Raewynne J Whiteley

"Follow me, and I will make you fishers of people." (Mark 1:17) When Jesus spoke those words to Simon and Andrew they set the pattern for all Christians from that day forward: called to follow Christ and to serve him in ministry. For the vast majority of Christians, that service will be expressed in the midst of their everyday lives; for some, however, it will be a particular call to leadership in the church through ordained ministry.

Discerning a call to ordained ministry is not something we do alone. While our own sense of call may develop through prayerful and obedient listening to God, it is up to the Church to recognize and affirm that call.

Speaking from a distinctively Australian perspective, Brad Billings offers a useful exploration of vocation and calling, and a guide to those wondering if they might be called to ordination in the Anglican tradition.

The Revd Dr Raewynne J Whiteley is the Warden, Wollaston Theological College, University of Divinity.

Dedication

Writing about calling, vocation and ministry inevitably recalls the circumstances of my own life. It reminds, in the first instance, of the magnitude of what it means to be called by God into the ordained ministry of his Church. This is gathered up in the solemn words from The Ordinal, spoken by the ordaining bishop to those who come to be ordained as priests – "we exhort you, in the Name of our Lord Jesus Christ, that you have in remembrance, into how high a dignity, and to how weighty an office and charge ye are called."

A life spent in service to God and his Church is always a life lived in community, in fellowship with God and with others. I have been especially fortunate to share that life of fellowship with my partner Karen, to whom I have been married for over thirty years now. We experienced the call to ministry together. We entered the path of discernment together, and walked it together, to the point of selection. Together we journeyed through the hard years of sacrifice, of study, formation and preparation. Together we served in the early years of two curacies, and then together led two different parishes, as co-workers and fellow labourers for the gospel. We continue to serve together today in the Diocese of Melbourne – me as a Bishop, and Karen as part of the diocesan Registry team.

Looking back over the years, and thinking about my own call and vocation in God's church, I know with gratitude that I have been immensely and extraordinarily blessed to be able to share all of this – the joys and the sorrows, the triumphs and the despairs – with Karen, to whom I dedicate this book. I would not have achieved whatever I have achieved, nor done the things I have done, both in ministry and in life, without her love, partnership and support.

Introduction

There is something intangible about the notion of "a call" and, it follows, there is something intangible about how a call is to be discerned, identified and understood. Further, the notion of a vocation, to which the concept of "a call" is often linked, is a term used widely in a number of different ways and contexts. Whilst they do go together in many ways, and are sometimes used interchangeably, there is a good case for distinguishing between the concepts of "call" and "vocation" in the context of Christian ministry. The call is primary, and has its source in the divine. It describes the prior act of God that gives rise to a vocation, and to how and in what circumstances that vocation is to be lived out. This is true of all Christian ministry, for all the baptised are called by God to live out their discipleship in a vocational way.

Of course, it is quite possible that a call may not be realised or acted on. It might not be recognised by the one to whom it comes, or by those entrusted with its discernment. It is quite possible also to claim, or experience, and in some cases even to live out, a vocation, without having ever been called. This can be further complicated in respect to the particular vocation of ordained ministry by the nexus between call and vocation on the one hand, and education and training (or what we might collectively describe as "formation") on the other hand. Traditionally, the discernment of, and subsequent affirmation of, a call to ordained ministry, preceded the requisite training and formation; but it is now common for this to be concurrent, or for the discernment of a call to take place after, and sometimes well after, a course of theological education and of training and formation in ministry has been undertaken and completed.

The intersection of vocation and call, and the associated movement toward professionalisation of the ordained ministry, introduces further complexity. To put it somewhat crudely, it is quite possible to educate and to train a person to do almost anything – to play a musical instrument, to learn a new language, to preach a sermon... It follows that it is possible to train a person to be a minister in the church of God, or at least to impart the academic and intellectual knowledge necessary, and to teach the skills required, to fulfil the duties of a Christian minister. But that, in itself, is never enough. It confers only an education and the requisite skills, knowledge and experience, together with an academic award. But this does not equate to a calling and a vocation. Only when the requisite intellectual knowledge, skills and experience are acquired in the context of the prior call of God, and only where the church in a corporate way recognises and endorses that the call is to ministry in an ordained capacity, is it possible that a person can be said to have both "a call" and "a vocation" to ordained ministry.

Articulating a call to ministry is no easy task. For good reason, an extensive piece of research in the Church of England found that "almost all people who had experienced a vocation to ministry struggled to describe it."[1] Rightly discerning a call to, and recognising a vocation in, Christian ministry in an ordained capacity, is even harder and will always be, to some extent, problematic. This is because it involves looking, very deeply, into the "heart" of a person, in the sense of the "heart" being a metaphor for the locus and essence of personhood; something only God can see with perfect and absolute clarity. It follows that this is no easy task for fallible humans, to the extent that there is a very real sense in which "the whole discernment process is about trying to put that which is inexpressible and seemingly unutterable into words."[2]

And yet, this process of discerning a call, and of recognising a vocation, is

---

[1] Sally Myers, 'New directions in voicing a vocation,' *Theology* 122 (2019), p. 179.

[2] Jonathan Lawson & Gordon Mursell, *Hearing the call: stories of young vocation* (London: SPCK, 2014), p, 12.

now, and has always been, both fundamental and critical in the context of the ordained ministry of the church. The importance of correctly discerning the will of God in these matters, insofar as that is humanly possible, is absolutely integral to the mission, health and sustaining of God's church, for "when it comes to the growth and life, or the decline and death, of the Church, the clergy are the key people."[3] This observation, grounded as it is in a careful study of church growth and decline in the Church of England, points to the reality that the quality of the ordained leadership is very often the critical (although not the only) factor, influencing church growth and decline.

The call to the vocation of ordained ministry continues, then, to be mission-critical, for in every generation the cry of the church is for leaders to inspire, encourage and equip the people of God to go out into their mission fields and to make known in word and in deed the good news about Jesus.

> Then Jesus went about all the cities and villages, teaching in their synagogues, and proclaiming the good news of the kingdom, and curing every disease and every sickness. When he saw the crowds, he had compassion for them, because they were harassed and helpless, like sheep without a shepherd. Then he said to his disciples, 'The harvest is plentiful, but the labourers are few; therefore ask the Lord of the harvest to send out labourers into his harvest.' (Matthew 9.35-38).

The purpose of this book is to provide guidance, and resources, for those who may be sensing that Jesus is calling them to participate in the harvest by offering themselves to be labourers for the gospel in an ordained capacity. In one sense, much of what follows is general in nature, in that it will concern the possibility of a calling and of a vocation to ordained ministry, how such a call and vocation may arise, and how it might be discerned and examined, both individually and corporately. The first part, consisting of the first four

---

3   Bob Jackson, *Hope for the church: contemporary strategies for growth* (London: Church House Publishing, 2002), p. 157.

chapters, examines these matters. The second part of this book is more specific, in that it examines the particularities of what it means to be called to the specific vocation of ordained ministry in the distinct context of the Anglican Church of Australia. In this, the two respective parts of this book are reflective of the critical, and very first, question put to every person who comes to be ordained as a deacon, and as a priest, in the Anglican Church of Australia. That critical question is twofold:

> Do you believe that you are truly called to this order and ministry of deacons/priests, being moved by the Holy Spirit to serve God and build up his people, according to the will of our Lord Jesus Christ *and* the order of this Anglican Church of Australia?[4]

Charles Sherlock in his *Australian Anglicans Worship*, identifies this question as the first of what he describes as the two "hurdle questions" asked of every candidate during the ordination service:

> For each 'order' there are two hurdle questions, which must receive positive responses before other questions about how candidates intend to exercise their ministry are put. The first concerns each candidate's acceptance of God's call… So deacons-elect are asked whether they be "moved by the Holy Spirit"… while they and priests-elect are asked if they are called "to this order and ministry according to the will of our Lord Jesus Christ and the order of this Anglican Church of Australia." The double condition is significant: acceptance of the Lord's will and the particularity of this Church stand together… The second 'hurdle' question concerns acceptance of the canonical Scriptures as the basic resource for Christian ministry and key criteria for Christian faith and life.[5]

---

4   APBA pp. 786, 794 – emphasis added.
5   *Australian Anglicans worship: performing APBA* (Broughton, 2020), p. 412.

Terminology

I am based in Melbourne, and the whole of my ministry, both in a lay and an ordained capacity, has been in the context of the Anglican Diocese of Melbourne. I am conscious, then, that I have, throughout this book, used terminology that is known to me, is natural to me and, at least in my experience, is in common use in my diocese. In addition to this, I have also used terms and language that have their source in the 1662 *Book of Common Prayer*, which may be unfamiliar to some readers.

I am conscious that it is the case that Anglicans across Australia, and beyond, do not use terminology consistently. For example, a "vicar" may also be referred to as a rector, incumbent, priest-in-charge, senior minister, or in another way, according to local custom across the diversity of the church. In some places the term "presbyter" is preferred to "priest" (The Ordinal in *A Prayer Book for Australia 1995* refers to "the ordination of priests also called presbyters"). I have used "clergyperson" in many places as a generic term for anyone who is ordained, largely because the designation "minister" on its own can properly refer to both ordained and lay persons. Whilst I am accustomed to referring to those involved in the selection process as "examining chaplains," in other places those who perform these functions might be known as "vocational advisers" or similar, or simply as selectors or interviewers.

There may well be other terms, and language, that are unfamiliar, which may be disliked or unpreferred by some readers, or which some might find jarring. None of this is intentional but is simply reflective of my own context and experience.

Abbreviations

APBA   *A Prayer Book for Australia 1995*

ARTICLE/S   The Thirty-Nine Articles of Religion

BCP   *The Book of Common Prayer 1662*

ORDINAL   (unless otherwise specified) *The Form and Manner of Making, Ordaining, and Consecrating of Bishops, Priests, and Deacons according to the Order of The Church of England* as included in and published in the *Book of Common Prayer 1662*

The Rt Revd Dr Bradly Billings
Pentecost 2022

PART A
VOCATION AND CALLING

1. Being – know yourself

The Lord said to Samuel, 'How long will you grieve over Saul? I have rejected him from being king over Israel. Fill your horn with oil and set out; I will send you to Jesse the Bethlehemite, for I have provided for myself a king among his sons.' Samuel said, 'How can I go? If Saul hears of it, he will kill me.' And the Lord said, 'Take a heifer with you, and say, "I have come to sacrifice to the Lord." Invite Jesse to the sacrifice, and I will show you what you shall do; and you shall anoint for me the one whom I name to you.' Samuel did what the Lord commanded and came to Bethlehem. The elders of the city came to meet him trembling, and said, 'Do you come peaceably?' He said, 'Peaceably; I have come to sacrifice to the Lord; sanctify yourselves and come with me to the sacrifice.' And he sanctified Jesse and his sons and invited them to the sacrifice. When they came, he looked on Eliab and thought, 'Surely the Lord's anointed is now before the Lord.' But the Lord said to Samuel, 'Do not look on his appearance or on the height of his stature, because I have rejected him; for the Lord does not see as mortals see; they look on the outward appearance, but the Lord looks on the heart.' (1 Samuel 16.1–7)

Vocation flows out of identity, and identity flows out of knowing the self. It is in understanding who we are that we begin to understand who we are called to be, and what we are called to do. These are the large and important questions (Who am I? Why am I here? What should I do with my life?) that human beings in every age and place have asked of themselves at some stage.

The answer is rooted in the very essence of personhood and may be found only in "the heart" – using the heart as a metaphor for the true nature and identity of the self, and as shorthand for that which makes me, *me* and you, *you*. Other than God, only the self really knows, and can really see, what truly lies within the heart.

Vocation

We often speak about ordained ministry in the church in terms of it being "a vocation" or "a calling" or both "a vocation and a calling". This is not surprising, as the two words are cognates; the English word "vocation" is derived from the Latin *vocare* which means "to call". These are terms that were once used predominately, if not exclusively, in religious contexts, and then more expansively in the so-called "helping professions" (doctors, nurses, social workers, etc.) and in the arts (musicians, writers, composers etc.). Even as early as the publication of Samuel Johnson's landmark *Dictionary of the English Language* in 1785, whilst vocation primarily meant "called by the will of God", it was already being used and applied to other trades and professions.[6]

The language of vocation is now widespread and familiar, and appears frequently in relation to the various occupations, jobs or careers a person may consider or have. So we have "vocational advisers" in education, in industry and in employment services, and we hear and speak of entering the workforce in terms of finding or pursuing our vocation. The *Oxford Dictionary* defines vocation as "a strong feeling of suitability for a particular career or occupation".[7] Consequently, vocation is now often associated closely with occupations, jobs and careers. People accept a job, or choose a

---

6 Robert Reiss, *The testing of vocation: 100 years of ministry selection in the Church of England* (London: Church House Publishing, 2013), p. 4.

7 *Oxford Dictionary of English* (Oxford: Oxford University Press, 3rd edn, 2010).

career, for all sorts of reasons. It may be to earn a good income, or to earn the best income they can in the circumstances; or perhaps because they consider it will bring fulfilment or happiness or both; and more altruistically, out of a desire to help others.

There is, however, a large and profound difference between choosing an occupation or pursuing a career for reasons such as those outlined above – however noble those reasons may be – and being called to live out a vocation in the context of the ordained ministry of the church. The vocation to ordained ministry arises, not out of a sense of what might be good or noble or worthwhile to do, nor what I may or may not be suited to do, but out of the prior call of God. It is about "becoming what God made you to be; and finding the place where you can most become that".[8] The salient point here is that, theologically, vocation, in terms of Christian ministry, has its source and origins in God, not in the human self. The human role in vocation resides in discerning what God is calling a person to do and to be.

Who am I?

Jesus once asked this question of his disciples, "Who am I?" The place was Caesarea Philippi, at the foot of Mount Hermon, in what is a beautiful natural environment located in the northern reaches of the Holy Land. In the trajectory of Mark's Gospel this is a key moment in relation to a key theme present throughout the narrative – the question of the identity of Jesus.

> Jesus went on with his disciples to the villages of Caesarea Philippi; and on the way he asked his disciples, "Who do people say that I am?" And they answered him, "John the Baptist; and others, Elijah; and still others, one of the prophets." He asked them, "But who do you say

---

8   Lawson & Mursell, *Hearing the Call*, p. 55.

that I am?" Peter answered him, "You are the Messiah." And he sternly ordered them not to tell anyone about him. (Mark 8.27–30)

In the same way that discovering the true identity of Jesus was necessary and essential for the disciples to exercise and fulfil the apostolic ministry into which they would subsequently be called, the discovering of one's vocation necessarily entails discovering and knowing one's own self. For the Christian today, as for the apostles before us, that self-understanding finds its source and meaning in rightly discerning and knowing the identity of the person of Jesus Christ, which then gives meaning and understanding to our own personhood "in Christ".

The German pastor and theologian Dietrich Bonhoeffer asked this question of himself in his Nazi prison cell toward the end of the Second World War, answering it in verse that is often repeated and reflected on, such is its beauty, simplicity and profundity.

Who am I? This or the Other?
Am I one person today and tomorrow another?
Am I both at once? A hypocrite before others,
and before myself a contemptible woebegone weakling?
Or is something within me still like a beaten army
fleeing in disorder from victory already achieved?
Who am I? They mock me, these lonely questions of mine.
Whoever I am, Thou knowest, O God, I am thine![9]

As Brian Rosner puts this simply and poignantly, in the context of biblical theology, "in order to know who you are, you have to know *whose you are*".[10]

---

9   *Letters and papers from prison* (London: SCM Press, 1952), p. 173.
10 *Known by God: A biblical theology of personal identity* (Grand Rapids: Zondervan, 2017), p. 131 (emphasis in the original).

Know thyself

The maxim "know thyself" was once carved into a column standing in the forecourt of the Temple of Apollo at Delphi, the magnificent locale and ruins of which can be visited today. The Greek traveller and writer Pausanias, who lived during the second century AD, wrote:

> In the fore-temple at Delphi are written maxims useful for the life of men, inscribed by those whom the Greeks say were sages… These sages, then, came to Delphi and dedicated to Apollo the celebrated maxims, "Know thyself" and "Nothing in excess".[11]

Xenophon demonstrates how integral this piece of ancient wisdom was to the Greek philosophical tradition, in attributing the advice below to Socrates:

> Is it not clear too that through self-knowledge men come to much good, and through self-deception to much harm? For those who know themselves, know what things are expedient for themselves and discern their own powers and limitations. And by doing what they understand, they get what they want and prosper: by refraining from attempting what they do not understand, they make no mistakes and avoid failure.[12]

Knowing oneself (Who am I?) informs both purpose (Why am I here?) and function (What will I do with my life?). Hence Gary Badcock begins his exploration of vocation and Christian theology with the prescient observation that the discernment of a vocation is very often the

---

11 Pausanias, *Description of Greece*, 10.24.1.
12 Xenophon, *Memorabilia* 4.2.

basic religious question people ask – "What will I do with the rest of my life?"[13] This is a question that can only really be answered with reference to the self, for it is a question of identity. That is, the question "Who am I?" is inseparable from the question "Who ought I to be?"[14] Bringing this into the context of ministry, Gordon Oliver observes: "Who on earth do you think you are?" and "What on earth do you think you are for?" are two basic questions every Christian must ask.[15]

The early church leader John Chrysostom, in his *On the Priesthood*, gives this timeless advice:

> In my opinion, then, though called and pressed by many, a man ought to pay no attention to them but he should first of all examine his own soul, and weigh everything carefully, and only then should he yield to pressure.[16]

The task of discernment begins then with the task of knowing and understanding one's own self in the context of Christian theology as a person "in Christ", out of the foundation of which, an understanding of "Why am I here?" and "What am I called to do?" arises. Put another way: "if vocation is about who God has called us to be as much as about what God has called us to do, the starting point for thinking about vocation lies precisely in who God made us to be, before we think about what it is that God has called us to do."[17]

---

13   *The way of life: theology of vocation* (Grand Rapids: Eerdmans 1998), p. 3.
14   Badcock, *The way of life*, p. 3.
15   Gordon Oliver, *Ministry without madness* (London: SPCK, 2012), p. 53.
16   St John Chrysostom, *Treatise on the Priesthood*, Book 4.
17   Chris Knights, 'Difficult texts: Mark 3.13-15: The nature of Christian vocation,' *Theology* 117 (2014), p. 279.

The first vocation

The very first vocation, and the primary call of every person, is to know and love God. The first vocation we have is, then, to be awakened and enlivened to the reality of the existence of the living God. As Karl Barth put this in his *Church Dogmatics* with both simplicity and clarity: "the purpose of a man's vocation is that he should become a Christian".[18] In the living out of this primary, fundamental and lifelong vocation, the one awakened to the existence of God – and whose own existence is in turn shaped by it – seeks to follow the example and teaching of the one who came to make God known, the Lord Jesus Christ. Hence, the essence of both the call and the vocation of all God's people is discipleship; to follow Christ. Theologically, this begins with the moment we first became aware of the existence of the love of God for us. Ritually and sacramentally that moment commences with baptism. The New Zealand Prayer Book puts it succinctly:

> We love because God first loves us.
> In baptism God declares that love;
> In Christ God calls us to respond.[19]

Baptism ritualises this reality and marks its commencement, and our response to it, which will continue for the duration of life. *Common Worship* (the Church of England) gives expression to this in these words, which are addressed to the newly baptised: "today God has touched you with his love… God now invites you on a life-long journey… to explore the way of Jesus and grow in friendship with God, in love for his

---

18   *Church Dogmatics*, Vol IV: *The Doctrine of Reconciliation*, Part 3.2, p. 521 (T&T Clark, 1961).

19   *A New Zealand Prayer Book: He Karakia Mihinare o Aotearoa* (Christchurch: Genesis, 1989), p. 383.

people, and in serving others".[20] All the baptised, that is all those who belong to Christ and are collectively Christ's body, share together in the vocation and mission of the church, each having within it their own part to play, for "there are varieties of gifts, but the same Spirit; and there are varieties of services, but the same Lord; and there are varieties of activities, but it is the same God who activates all of them in everyone". (1 Corinthians 12.4–6) All the baptised are collectively the body of Christ, and individually members of it. (1 Corinthians 12.27)

> Our Lord Jesus Christ summons us all to obedience and discipleship. In baptism we are called to be a royal priesthood, a people belonging to God, to make Christ known in the world.[21]

The language here points to the biblical notion of the "priesthood of all believers" (1 Peter 2.9) and reminds us that the vocation of the baptised is to live out their respective discipleship in the context of day-to-day life, over the course of that life. For the person of Christian faith, it is fundamental that the primary consideration in regard to the question of "What should I do with my life?" is, whatever I ultimately choose to do, even if that choice is somehow made for me, must be capable of serving the mission of Christ. This can occur in almost any context and in all manner of ways, for all of life is discipleship and, therefore, a life of applied Christian ministry, broadly defined.

The theologian Paul Avis, who is one of the foremost scholars and commentators on the theology of the church today, reminds us that, though bishops and laypeople may, from the outside looking in, be thought to be "at the opposite ends of the spectrum of Christian callings",

---

20 *Common Worship: Services and prayers for the Church of England* (London: Church House Publishing, 2000), p. 359.
21 APBA 'The Ordination of Priests,' p. 793.

there is, theologically speaking, "no such spectrum".[22] As he goes on to describe, this is because, "considered biblically and theologically, the church is a perfectly level playing field," with everyone being called into the ordering of the community of the baptised to participate in the service of God's mission.[23] It is important, then, to understand that it is not the case that only the ordained are called to a ministry or to have a vocation, for "the laity are just as fully ecclesial persons as the ordained are".[24] All Christians are called to follow Christ in the way of discipleship, and all have a vocation to ministry. The questions are, where and how this is to be expressed in the lived experience of one's discipleship. Within the life of discipleship exists the possibility of a calling into many different vocational ministries, one possibility of which is a calling into the specific vocation of the ordained ministry.

Being and doing

As we have already seen, "ministry is partly being and partly doing" and "trying to disentangle the two is impossible".[25] In Mark's gospel (3.13–15) Jesus calls the twelve to "be with him" and then sends them out "to do" something (preach and proclaim). This suggests that vocational ministry has a dual emphasis on the relationship with Christ (on being "with him") and on doing something on his behalf (being "sent" by him).[26]

Whilst from the outside looking in, ordained ministry looks like it is about "doing" – and certainly there is always much to do – in reality, a

---

22 'The Roles of the Ecclesial Orders in the Governance of the Church,' *Ecclesiology* 18 (2022), p. 3.
23 Avis, 'The Roles of the Ecclesial Orders in the Governance of the Church,' p. 3.
24 Avis, 'The Roles of the Ecclesial Orders in the Governance of the Church,' p. 3.
25 Andrew Pratt, *Practical skills for ministry* (London: SCM press, 2010), p. 1.
26 Knights, 'Difficult texts,' p. 278.

large and critical part of inhabiting ordained ministry is about "being". It is about knowing who I am, who I am becoming and who I will be. John-Francis Friendship begins his treatise on the inner life of the priest with the observation that "ministry can be experienced as a never-ending round of 'doing' and, in my experience, the need for simply 'being' can be neglected – usually to the detriment of the minister and ministry".[27]

The exemplar in this is Jesus himself, who often withdrew to a place of solitude and quietness, after a busy period of doing, to reflect and pray, and to simply "be" in the presence of God.

> In the morning, while it was still very dark, he got up and went out to a deserted place, and there he prayed. (Mark 1.35)
>
> Now during those days he went out to the mountain to pray; and he spent the night in prayer to God. (Luke 6.12)
>
> He said to them, 'Come away to a deserted place all by yourselves and rest a while.' (Mark 6.31)

The nexus between "being" and "doing" raises the significant matter of the – sometimes apparent, sometimes concealed and sometimes not transparent – disparity between who we are and the role we are occupying. This goes to both how we see ourselves and how others see us. The advice of Andrew Pratt is salient: "know yourself, but you also need to be yourself... God has not called you because you are like someone else, but because you are you!"[28] Hence advice of Polonius to Laertes in Shakespeare's *Hamlet* is often quoted:

> Neither a borrower nor a lender be;
> For loan oft loses both itself and friend,

---

27   *Enfolded in Christ: The inner life of a priest* (Norwich: Canterbury Press, 2018), p. xxi.
28   *Practical skills for ministry*, p. 8.

> And borrowing dulls the edge of husbandry.
> This above all: to thine own self be true,
> And it must follow, as the night the day,
> Thou canst not then be false to any man.[29]

In the context of a vocation to ordained ministry, it is the knowing of, and being honest with, the self that gives rise to a sense of being who I am in Christ, that in turn gives rise to the firm conviction about what it is that I am called by God to do with my life. For the one genuinely called to a vocation in ordained ministry, the offering of that vocation for the discernment and testing of the church is not something that might be done if and when I might get around to it, and it is not something that I might "try" one day; but conversely, it is something that *must* be done in order to be true to (honest with) "thine own self".

> You did not choose me but I chose you. And I appointed you to go and bear fruit, fruit that will last, so that the Father will give you whatever you ask him in my name. (John 15.16)

Born for this

The vocation we each have as a Christian and as a disciple of Jesus is always much more than what we *might* do, or *aspire* to do, or what we *are* doing at any given time. Vocation arises out of who we are and goes to our very heart and being. It is something we do in order to be who, and whose, we are.

> There is a huge difference between a vocation and a job. A job is what we hold to earn money to meet economic needs. A vocation… is what

---

[29] *Hamlet* Act 1, scene 3, 75–77.

we are called to do with our life's energy… We do not choose a vocation, rather it chooses us.[30]

This is to understand vocation and calling in a sense that it is so rooted in God that it can only be discerned by knowing God and by knowing the self deeply and intimately. When it emerges, and is recognised rather than found, residing in the very core of our being, already existing there because it has been planted there by God waiting for the moment of discovery, the emergence and discovery of that vocation gives our life further meaning and purpose, because it tells us what we are being called do, having already discovered and known who, and whose, we are.

For some people these two things – the discovery of the existence and reality of God and of the love of God for us, and the discovery of the vocation God is calling us into – are simultaneous events; whilst for many others these two things may be separated in time, and sometimes an extended passage of time. However it comes about, and when, the experience of finding and recognising the vocation into which the individual disciple is called by God causes the one who finds it to say with Jesus, "for this reason I was born and came into the world". (John 18.37) For many disciples, the vast majority in fact, that vocation will not be to the ordained ministry. But for some it will be.

In some profound way, I only really fully knew and recognised what I was born to do, and heard myself saying those words ("for this reason I was born") internally, upon being commissioned as vicar to my second parish, some years after my initial selection and formation as a candidate for ordination, and long after the ordination itself. On reflection, I expect it was the weight of expectation and the nature of that particular position and the many joys and challenges it presented and which I knew lay ahead, that caused me to think, pray and ask whether I had rightly discerned God

---

30   Lawson & Mursell, *Hearing the call*, p, 94

calling and leading me through the selection process, the ordination itself, and into this particular role. I recall standing before the congregation of the faithful who had gathered for the first Sunday service I was to lead in that place, opening my arms in a gesture of welcome, and giving the liturgical greeting ("the Lord be with you") as I had done many times before in different places filled with different people, and hearing within, for the first time really, even as the response ("and also with you") echoed around the church – "you belong here, you were born for this, I am with you". It was, and remains, a very rare, powerful experience of the work of the Holy Spirit, that has sustained and empowered me in ministry many times since. That experience was the rock and foundation on which I built my ministry in that place and, more than that, it has become the rock and foundation on which my ordained ministry has been subsequently constructed, for I found myself coming back to that experience time and time again, reliving that moment and hearing those words – "you belong here, you were born for this, I am with you" – especially in times of great difficulty, pain and struggle.

2. When God speaks your name

But Mary stood weeping outside the tomb. As she wept, she bent over to look into the tomb; and she saw two angels in white, sitting where the body of Jesus had been lying, one at the head and the other at the feet. They said to her, 'Woman, why are you weeping?' She said to them, 'They have taken away my Lord, and I do not know where they have laid him.' When she had said this, she turned round and saw Jesus standing there, but she did not know that it was Jesus. Jesus said to her, 'Woman, why are you weeping? For whom are you looking?' Supposing him to be the gardener, she said to him, 'Sir, if you have carried him away, tell me where you have laid him, and I will take him away.' Jesus said to her, 'Mary!' She turned and said to him in Hebrew, 'Rabbouni!' (which means Teacher). Jesus said to her, 'Do not hold on to me, because I have not yet ascended to the Father. But go to my brothers and say to them, "I am ascending to my Father and your Father, to my God and your God."' Mary Magdalene went and announced to the disciples, 'I have seen the Lord'; and she told them that he had said these things to her. (John 20.11–18)

The account of the resurrection of Jesus in John's Gospel is dramatic and compelling. Its focus falls on the person of Mary, who, we are told as the narrative begins, stands weeping outside the tomb. For Mary, it seems, all hope has been lost with the death and burial of the one she and the other disciples had called "the Lord". But as we know, looking back in time from this side of the defining event in salvation history, the resurrection of Jesus Christ from the dead, the gospel story does not end with the death and burial of Jesus. It is only just beginning. Mary, distressed, alone and confused, is about to stand, not as she believes weeping before a tomb containing the dead body of Jesus, but in the very presence of the risen Lord. Unable to see through the fog of her present circumstances and grief, Mary does not recognise this visitation. In fact, such is her grief and confusion, she supposes the risen Lord to be "the gardener". It calls to mind how often we might miss the presence of the risen Lord ourselves in some way, and those times when perhaps we too might have mistaken the risen Lord for "the gardener" or another. It is only when Jesus speaks a single word, her name ("Jesus said to her, Mary!"), that Mary finally realises she stands in the very presence of the risen Lord himself. And this is what discerning a call is all about! It is about hearing the voice of the divine speak your name (however that may happen).

> But now thus says the Lord,
> he who created you, O Jacob,
> he who formed you, O Israel:
> Do not fear, for I have redeemed you;
> I have called you by name, you are mine. (Isaiah 43.1)

For most of us, inclusive of me, this may not be as dramatic and as audible and as overwhelming as the call heard and received by Mary in the garden on the first Easter morning. But however it happens, it remains axiomatic that in order to *respond* to a call, you must first *be* called. That is, God must speak your name, somehow and in some way. Further, that call must be heard and received by the self. This entails listening, very carefully and very deeply, to God, and being alert to the activity of the Holy Spirit in the midst of the busy-ness, noise and clutter of everyday life.

He said, 'Go out and stand on the mountain before the Lord, for the

Lord is about to pass by.' Now there was a great wind, so strong that it was splitting mountains and breaking rocks in pieces before the Lord, but the Lord was not in the wind; and after the wind an earthquake, but the Lord was not in the earthquake; and after the earthquake a fire, but the Lord was not in the fire; and after the fire a sound of sheer silence. When Elijah heard it, he wrapped his face in his mantle and went out and stood at the entrance of the cave. Then there came a voice to him that said, 'What are you doing here, Elijah?' (1 Kings 19.11–13)

This is not often, or even always, something we can do alone. As Jonathan Lawson and Gordon Mursell observe, "we can sometimes only 'hear' things when they have been received by another – when they have been externalized, said out loud".[31] They give this further, prescient advice:

> It is therefore a really important prerequisite if you are considering your sense of vocation that you talk to someone you trust, who will take seriously and handle sensitively what you tell them. Hearing someone talk about their sense of vocation, particularly for the first time, is like receiving a precious and fragile gift.[32]

Finally, and perhaps most problematically of all in respect to a call to ordained ministry, the call of God to the individual must also be recognised and heard by one, and usually more than one, representative persons on behalf of the people of God ("the church").

---

[31] Lawson & Mursell, *Hearing the call*, p, 4.
[32] Ibid, p. 4.

Call

It can be helpful to begin with the broad understanding of vocation in the Hebrew Bible (our Old Testament) as being, generally, about the call of God to a select person, whilst in the New Testament vocation is more about the call that comes from God to all persons to follow a specific person, Jesus.[33]

There are many "call stories" in the Scriptures, both in the Hebrew Bible and in the New Testament; from the call of the patriarchs Abraham and Moses, to the prophets Isaiah, Jeremiah, and Ezekiel, to the call of John the Baptist, Mary, and Jesus himself. Jesus, in turn, called the first disciples to follow him, providing us with a powerful narrative of encounter and call that resonates down through the centuries.

> As he walked by the Sea of Galilee, he saw two brothers, Simon, who is called Peter, and Andrew his brother, casting a net into the lake—for they were fishermen. And he said to them, 'Follow me, and I will make you fish for people.' Immediately they left their nets and followed him. As he went from there, he saw two other brothers, James son of Zebedee and his brother John, in the boat with their father Zebedee, mending their nets, and he called them. Immediately they left the boat and their father, and followed him. (Matthew 4.18–22)

This call could scarcely be more simple, existing in the imperative "follow me" and coupled with the promise of equipping ("and I will make you fish for people"). This is a call so compelling, that it is immediately and irresistibly responded to, despite the cost, which is substantial, for it demanded Peter and Andrew, and James and John, to leave their homes, their families, and their occupations. This is a call that required them, and others after them to whom the same call would come, "to give up their professions and to devote

---

33   B Ferguson & D.F. Wright (Eds), *New Dictionary of Theology* (Leicester, 1988), p. 711.

their entire time and energy to be to be trained by Jesus to become 'fishers of people' and then to be sent into the world to proclaim the news of the kingdom of God and of Jesus the Messiah and Saviour".[34]

In his exegesis of this pivotal text, Donald Hagner emphasises that the call of Jesus is rooted in the prior activity of God.

> The invitation of Jesus amounts to a demand based on electing grace. That is, the disciples have been chosen by Jesus to follow after him ("come"). The invitation is accompanied by the promise that Jesus will equip them ("make") for the work to which he calls them… The idea of "following after" another stems from the Jewish background of the rabbis and their disciples, where imitation of the master's example, and not only his teaching, is given great importance. The crucial difference from the rabbinic practice is that here the master, not the would-be disciples, takes the initiative to establish the relationship.[35]

Applying this text and the theology that arises out of it to ordained ministry today, we can sum this up rather simplistically, but I think rightly, in this way. The call is primary and essential: out of it vocation emerges, and then is built over the course of all that follows; for the vocation, once discerned and once confirmed by the church in ordination, is lifelong. The Roman Catholic theologian Gerald O'Collins, noting that Jesus called his disciples from an already existing community of disciples and from among the number of the existing faithful, sees a similar if not exact parallel to the way "those to be ordained for ministry are called out of the wider community" and "chosen".[36]

---

34 Eckhard J. Schnabel, *Paul the missionary: realities, strategies and methods* (Downers Grove, IL: InterVarsity Press, 2008), p. 383.

35 *Matthew 1-13* (Word Biblical Commentary 33A; Dallas, Word, 1993), p. 76.

36 'Jesus and the ordained ministry: A Christocentric view of priesthood,' *Irish Theological Quarterly* 76 (2011), p. 24.

Further, the call to ordained ministry, once known and experienced, and having been endorsed and executed by the church, never disappears. It is always present, always needed. It is the well of "living water" being constantly refreshed, that sustains and energises the vocation.

> On the last day of the festival, the great day, while Jesus was standing there, he cried out, 'Let anyone who is thirsty come to me, and let the one who believes in me drink. As the scripture has said, "Out of the believer's heart shall flow rivers of living water".' Now he said this about the Spirit, which believers in him were to receive; for as yet there was no Spirit, because Jesus was not yet glorified. (John 7.37–39)

The disciples, of course, encountered the very person of Jesus as he walked along the shores of the Sea of Galilee and summoned them to follow him. There was nothing subjective about this call. The very Son of God was standing in their presence commanding them to follow him. But how do we, as disciples living many centuries on this side of the life, death, resurrection and ascension of Jesus, know and recognise the call of Jesus to follow him into the ordained ministry of the church? For those who seek to discern the call of God today, this is an inherently subjective question, one that is asked by every prospective ordained minister, and one which will have as many answers, or at least attempts at answers, as there are prospective ordained ministers. In light of this, how are those given responsibility on behalf of the church – to objectively discern, assess and determine a calling into ordained ministry – to go about the task of doing that? Again, the answer will vary, depending on the procedures and the processes in place, and on the person or persons tasked with this duty.

What we can say, with certainty, is that both the subjective call experienced by the individual, and the objective recognition of that call by "the church" through the agency of its representative person or persons, must both be present and affirmed in respect to the discernment and validation of any call and of every vocation to the ordained ministry.

The subjective call

For Matt Woodcock, the call came as he drove along a motorway in northern England.

> For St Paul it was the Road to Damascus, for me it was the A19 to Selby. Why God chose that day, that moment, that stretch of carriageway, I don't know. I wasn't feeling particularly spiritual or anything. I was on my way to cover a case at Selby Magistrates' Court for the *York Press*. I don't remember exactly what I was doing when everything went weird… Suddenly my head began to swim, and my stomach turned over. My Ford Fiesta became difficult to control. I pulled into a layby to try to compose myself. As strange as it sounds – and as hard as it is to convey in words – I felt an overwhelming sense that God had something he wanted to tell me.[37]

For others the experience will be less dramatic, and unable to be located in a single time or place, in that it may arise out of an inner conviction accumulating over time until it becomes impossible to ignore. Charles Richardson, in his introduction to *This is our Calling*, writes: "the 'voice of God within' is being heard, but as variously as our personalities, cultures and situations will allow. Describing this 'voice' or 'call' from God is a metaphor for the many ways in which we experience the things of God".[38] A call, having its source and origin in God, may be traced to a core experience, often spiritual

---

37 *Becoming Reverend: A diary* (London: Church House Publishing, 2016), p. 3.
38 *This is our calling* (London: SPCK, 2004), p. xvi.

in nature, whether that experience is in the distant past or not reachable at all in the present.[39] It may be that the moment is immediately and vividly identifiable, as for Matt Woodcock. Or it may be that there is no moment to be identified at all, only an inner conviction that has no identifiable origin other than that it is experienced as being from or of God. Put another way, an experience of God is often, at the same time, an experience of God's call.[40]

Clearly, the entire notion of receiving and rightly discerning, hearing and responding to a call is a subjective thing. It may well consist only in an intangible event or conviction that is only ever truly knowable to the individual who experiences it. Yet it is essential there be a subjective call, and that the one professing to be called both experiences this and testifies to it. The first two questions asked by the ordaining Bishop of the candidates about to be ordained Deacon in The Ordinal are, "Do you trust that you are inwardly moved by the Holy Ghost to take upon you this Office and Ministration, to serve God for the promoting of his glory, and the edifying of this people?" and "Do you think you are truly called, according to the will of our Lord Jesus Christ, and the due order of this Realm, to the Ministry of the Church?" In the Ordering of Priests, the first question asked of the candidate is "Do you think in your heart, that you be truly called, according to the will of our Lord Jesus Christ, and the Order of this Church of England, to the Order and Ministry of Priesthood?"

The objective call

The early church leader Cyprian, who lived in North Africa in the third century AD, in a strongly worded treatise on the ordination of new clergy, insisted that a "priest should be chosen in the presence of the people under

---

39 Badcock, *The way of life*, p. 73.
40 Badcock, *The way of life*, p. 74.

the eyes of all, and should be approved worthy and suitable by public judgement and testimony".[41]

This points to the custom that, from the very beginning, the people of God, collectively "the church," had a significant responsibility and role in the discernment of new ministers. In the early chapters of the Acts of the Apostles, it is the community who select and appoint those who will be set aside for a ministry of service from within their own number.

> Now during those days, when the disciples were increasing in number, the Hellenists complained against the Hebrews because their widows were being neglected in the daily distribution of food. And the twelve called together the whole community of the disciples and said, "It is not right that we should neglect the word of God in order to wait on tables. Therefore, friends, select from among yourselves seven men of good standing, full of the Spirit and of wisdom, whom we may appoint to this task, while we, for our part, will devote ourselves to prayer and to serving the word." What they said pleased the whole community, and they chose Stephen, a man full of faith and the Holy Spirit, together with Philip, Prochorus, Nicanor, Timon, Parmenas, and Nicolaus, a proselyte of Antioch. They had these men stand before the apostles, who prayed and laid their hands on them. (Acts 6.1–6)

It is the prophets and teachers in the church at Antioch who rightly discern that Barnabas and Saul were called by God to a ministry of evangelism, and who subsequently lay hands on them and send them out into the mission field.

> Now in the church at Antioch there were prophets and teachers: Barnabas, Simeon who was called Niger, Lucius of Cyrene, Manaen

---

41 *Epistles* 67.4.

a member of the court of Herod the ruler, and Saul. While they were worshipping the Lord and fasting, the Holy Spirit said, 'Set apart for me Barnabas and Saul for the work to which I have called them.' Then after fasting and praying they laid their hands on them and sent them off. (Acts 13.1–3)

Whilst it is essential that there be an inner call, the emphasis on, and the importance vested in, the inner call experienced by the individual self is a relatively recent phenomenon. Francis Dewar argues that the church has, in fact, unhelpfully exalted the "inner conviction" of a call to ordained ministry, arguing that the call comes, not exclusively to, or from within, the individual self, but corporately, to and from the church.[42] Similarly Bishop Walter Frere (1863–1938), who helped co-found the Community of the Resurrection at Mirfield in northern England, thought it a "disastrous mistake" that the Church had come to lay all but exclusive emphasis on the interior call; whilst H. L. Goudge, then professor of divinity at Oxford University, wrote in 1938 that the presence of the first question put to those to be ordained deacon in The Ordinal (Do you believe that you are truly called to this order and ministry?) was "nothing less than a disaster."[43]

These strongly worded statements remind us to guard against emphasising or exalting the interior or subjective call, over the exterior or objective call. It is one thing for a person to experience and articulate a sense of calling to ordained ministry arising out of an inner conviction, even one very strongly articulated and very strongly felt; but another thing entirely for the church in a corporate way to also recognise and affirm that call. This is not an invention of the Anglican Church, nor by any means a recent phenomenon. In his extensive study of the laws of Christian churches of all denominations, from the Roman Catholic

---

42   *Called or collared? An alternative approach to vocation* (London: SPCK, 2000), p. 14.
43   Reiss, *The testing of vocation*, pp. 13, 16.

to the Orthodox and Protestant churches, Norman Doe finds that, in every tradition, "candidates for ordination must be called by God and their vocation is tested by the church through a process of selection, examination and training."[44]

Decision

Any person professing a call and a vocation to ordained ministry must be able to give an emphatic "yes" to the question "Do you believe that you are truly called to this order and ministry… being moved by the Holy Spirit to serve God and build up his people, according to the will of our Lord Jesus Christ?" And, critically, the representatives of the church charged with the responsibility of recognising a call and discerning a vocation to ordained ministry on behalf of the people of God in that part of the Christian family, must be able to also say "yes" to the question, "Can you assure us that this person is suited by their learning and godly living to minister as a Deacon in the household of God, to the glory of God?"[45] These two affirmations ("yes"), one to the conviction and belief of the individual that he or she is truly called, and one by the representatives of the church in recognition of the existence of that call coupled with an assurance as to the candidate's suitability and learning, are the two sides of the one vocational coin.

The moment of decision arrives when a person who experiences an inner conviction of a calling into the vocation of ordained ministry, which cannot be any longer postponed or ignored, acts on that inner conviction or subjective call, by making the decision to submit that calling to the formal testing and proving of the church. The church does this in an objective way, usually through a formal selection process, administered by representative

---

44 *Christian Law: Contemporary principles* (Cambridge University Press, 2013), p. 116.
45 The two questions are adapted from APBA, 'The Ordination of Deacons,' pp. 784, 786.

persons charged with the responsibility of testing, proving and ultimately discerning, a potential call to the vocation of ordained ministry.

This decision is a large and important one. It is potentially life changing. It places the one making that decision in a very vulnerable position, for it opens up the possibility that the church may not be able to reciprocate the "yes" experienced subjectively by the self, but may have to say, having applied its objective process of discernment, "no" or "not yet". As the Reformer Thomas Beccon (ca. 1511–1567), in his *Catechesis*, advised those desiring to offer themselves for ordained ministry, they ought to do so, not out of ambition or desire for worldly gain but should "submit… to the judgement of the congregation, either to be admitted, or to be refused."

For the one truly called, however, this is a decision that must be taken, for it is about obedience. As Chris Knights suggests, the "heart of vocation is not calling but obedience," for the moment of decision "is about discerning what we are called to do or not do (alongside who we are called to be) and then obeying that call."[46] The compelling nature of the call to obey is such that, it must be followed by the subjective self, even at the risk of the answer of the objective decision makers on behalf of the church being "no".

But why?

We should not leave this section on the subjective and objective call, and the moment of decision, without considering the question "why?". That is, why offer yourself for ordination in the first place? Or, why would you (or anyone in fact) want to be ordained? It was the most common question I was asked throughout my period of training and formation, not only by occasional acquaintances and people I was meeting for the first time who had enquired about what it was I did or what I was studying and training

---

46   'Difficult texts,' p. 279.

to do; but also by people within my network of family and friends, both within the church and beyond it, many of whom had known I had previously entered law school and harboured aspirations for the legal profession. One person I recall meeting at a function or dinner party even put the question rather bluntly, asking incredulously across the table, "But why throw away a career in the law to be a priest?" Why indeed?

The conclusion above, that it is about obedience to the calling of God, of course explains this theologically, and makes sense to people of faith. But many of those called to ministry find this very difficult to articulate and explain to those in their social circles, and to disappointed or aghast family and friends. Further, the "why?" question is often one of the first, if not the first, asked of an aspiring candidate for ordination by a diocesan vocations adviser or bishop, who may enquire gently at the first meeting, after the pleasantries and getting to you know small talk has been exhausted, "So, why are you here?" Or perhaps more bluntly, "Why do you want to be ordained?"

Why indeed! Alan Billings (who was ordained in the 1960s) notes at the beginning of his highly engaging treatise on ordained ministry, "for as I long as I can remember, ordained ministry has been facing a crisis – or so people have claimed."[47] The crisis is generally expressed as being in terms of the poor morale of the clergy and the broader church, exacerbated by the increasing marginalisation and rapid pace of secularisation, that often produces anxieties around the uncertain future of the institutional church. Further, the clerical profession is one in which there is no real career pathway of the nature found in many other professions. Bishops are usually elected or chosen, often for reasons that are not entirely related to who might be the best person for the role at that time. A clergyperson who attains the position of a vicar, or a priest in charge, or senior chaplain to an institution, or similar, has often gone as far as they can in the clerical hierarchy and in terms of the stipend they will receive. This is not the whole

---

47 *Making God possible: the task of ordained ministry present and future* (London: SPCK, 2010), p. 3.

story of course, but is a truism confronted by many during the course of their ordained ministry.

All this returns us to the fundamental question "why?". It can be surprising how often this question is avoided, and never asked or returned to, once a person is ordained and sent out into the mission field to minister. Having successfully articulated a vocation, and satisfactorily answered the question "why?" at the time of their selection, some seemingly consider the answer they gave at that time can now be safely ignored and forgotten. But this is not the case, for if a person loses sight of the very reasons for which they offered to serve God in the ordained ministry in the first place, they may very well, and will probably inevitably, lose sight of their purpose. And that can only lead to a loss of morale, despair, and even burnout, in the very worst of cases leading to a withdrawal from ordained ministry altogether.

3. Qualities and characteristics

Having decided that there is a call to serve in the ordained ministry and having further determined that this call to service is in the context of the Anglican Church of Australia, it is appropriate to further consider, at this point, what the particular characteristics and qualities those charged with the task of discerning a vocation to ordained ministry will be seeking to identify in aspirants.

This is not a straightforward task, and not as clear as it sometimes is in other professions. The question in other contexts may be one of skill or ability – one can either perform the skills required of the profession, trade, or occupation, or not. The reality is, the disciples called by Jesus were not natural or logical choices, looking through a secular or worldly lens. Neither was the towering figure of early Christianity, Paul, who was certainly found wanting when compared (as he was by the Corinthians in particular), to the travelling rhetoricians and great orators who had so wowed Roman audiences at his time. "For they say, 'His letters are weighty and strong, but his bodily presence is weak, and his speech contemptible" (2 Corinthians 10.10). As Stephen Conway observes, the same could easily be said of those whom God called and chose to be his vessels in the pages of the Hebrew Bible, for "any personality profile of the prophets does not suggest that they would find selection for ministries within the Church satisfying or successful."[48]

This reminds us that the call of God may come to anyone, both

---

48 'The call for others,' in Charles Richardson (ed), *This is our calling* (London: SPCK, 2004), p. 35.

the likely and the unlikely, and even the extremely unlikely. Further, we know that if God calls, God also equips, giving with that call the necessary and needful gifts of grace for its living out. No candidate, however impressive, ever comes to a selection panel as the finished and complete article, for we are all a work in progress in the divine economy, constantly being formed and re-formed to be who we are and who God is calling us to be. For this very reason selectors should be, and usually are, seeking to discern potential; whether the candidate has sufficient potential to be formed, shaped and proved for ordination at a later, and often a much later, time.

The long history of the church and its ordained ministries does, however, provide considerable insight into the sort of qualities and characteristics that are going to be required of a person exploring a vocation to the ordained ministry, and which will be needed to sustain a lifelong commitment to that vocation. So it is good, helpful and right that prospective and discerning candidates become, at an early stage in their own process of discernment, acquainted with that which will be asked and required of them if they are ultimately ordained, with a view to determining and judging whether this is, in fact, truly the life for them.

Suitability

Suitability is a nebulous concept, difficult to define, and therefore even more difficult to discern. There are, however, some fundamentals, some set out in canon law, that are in the nature of minimum requirements. In brief, an aspirant for ordination must:

- Have attained a minimum age of 23 for ordination as deacon, and of 24 for ordination as priest;

- Be baptised, and either confirmed or received into communicant membership of the Anglican Church of Australia;

- Be of good character;

- Have completed appropriate training in theological and ministerial formation, and have sufficient knowledge of Holy Scripture and the liturgical practices of the Anglican Church;

- Have been an active, worshipping member of the Anglican Church for at least 12 months.

These minimum requirements are clear, and reflect the historic canon law of the early and medieval church, as well as the longstanding practice of the Church of England and other Anglican Churches around the world. But they are in the nature of minimum legal stipulations, and leave much else to the individual and collective discernment of those involved in the selection process. Whilst it can be straightforward to determine evidence of age, proof of baptism and confirmation or reception through the production of relevant documents, determining "good character" in an objective way, and determining the sufficiency, or otherwise, of a candidate's knowledge of Holy Scripture and the liturgical practices of the Anglican Church, is clearly more nuanced. Further, the extent of "appropriate" training and formation prior to ordination is malleable, and can, and often does, mean different things in different contexts. Some may understand a candidate's extensive life and ministerial experience to be appropriate in itself, for instance, whilst others may insist on an undergraduate or postgraduate degree with successful completion of specific subjects such as New Testament Greek among several others.

In essence, suitability is an intangible criteria and test, just as the very notion of a call and of a vocation to ordained ministry is often intangible and difficult to define objectively. In practice, a whole range of factors will shape and inform the question of an individual candidate's suitability, usually after having the benefit of an input from several persons or groups of persons. There will be, and often are, objective tests, such as evidence of sustained participation in worship, references as to character from significant people, ministerial placements that will entail some accountabilities and reporting, and completion of a course of study usually for academic award. But successful completion of any or all of this, and more, will not necessarily surmount to suitability. In a process of discernment, by and through which a candidate is tested and considered for their suitability for ordination, spiritual insight will have a role to play. This may result in a candidate being determined unsuitable for ordained ministry, in circumstances whereby the selectors or their representative or representatives may not be in a position to provide much detail as to why.

Capacity

Whilst sometimes expressed in earlier canon law in terms that would not be used today, a fundamental, and often overlooked quality, is that a candidate for ordination must demonstrate "the physical and mental capacity to minister".[49] The historic antecedents of this requirement are found in the direction in canon law that the ordaining bishop must be satisfied that the candidate has the physical and mental capacity to minister effectively in what is an often demanding, and intended to be lifelong, vocation. In modern selection processes, this is typically met by requiring a candidate to undergo a standard workplace medical check, usually with their general practitioner, to ensure they are in robust enough physical health to carry out the duties of an ordained minister; and by requiring the candidate to

---

49   *Canon Concerning Holy Orders 2004* s 5(1)(j).

be assessed psychologically by a qualified person, who may make use of a range of clinical tools to determine that the psychological outlook of the candidate does not present any barrier to them ministering effectively, and that the strategies they have in place to nurture and sustain their own mental health will be sufficient to withstand the many rigours of ordained ministry.

The historic test of "physical and mental capacity" has become very prominent in recent years, with the church, rightly, investing intentionally in psychological evaluations that seek to determine that the personal and behavioural characteristics of a candidate do not raise any "red flags" as to both their suitability in general, in respect to the protection of children and vulnerable people, and in what might be more broadly called safeguarding.

At its heart, the test of physical and mental capacity is about wellbeing – specifically, the personal wellbeing of the individual candidate, and their immediate family, as well as the corporate wellbeing of the church and its witness to the world. The intention underlying this is to desist from placing a person who is, for whatever reason, physically or mentally, or both physically and mentally, ill-equipped to cope, into a position that will be foreseeably detrimental to their own personal wellbeing. In short, it is about the duty of care owed by the church both to the candidate, and to itself.

Spiritual Maturity

Any person professing to be called to ordained ministry in the church must exhibit spiritual maturity as a fundamental quality. Spiritual maturity is, however, an elusive thing. It can be hard to know what it looks like. It is not so much a matter of being schooled and learned in Christian orthodoxy, as important as that is. Nor is spiritual maturity to be found in having settled the great questions of life, faith and meaning, or by claiming that all doubt about these matters has been eliminated. It is found in the act of believing, and in the living out of that belief – even in the midst of the usual doubts, worries, failures and weaknesses of human life. The only way to really identify spiritual maturity is to observe it. In short, we will only really know and recognise it when we see it.

Conversely, and perhaps somewhat presciently, we might intuitively know and recognise the inverse, spiritual immaturity, when we observe it. For this reason the ordination selection process relies heavily on the observations and assertions of others, usually many others, concerning the candidate, in respect to both the candidate's sense of calling and vocation, and the extent to which the candidate exhibits the spiritual maturity that is reasonably to be expected of a person being called to serve the church in the ordained ministry.

However it is to be understood and recognised, spiritual maturity is an absolutely fundamental quality for any prospective candidate for ordination, and of all the ordained:

> When we see a life that radiates the love and peace of God, mature in the Spirit, nothing is more attractive or converting. When maturity is lacking in those who are ordained, no amount of correct teaching or liturgical competence or mission planning can make up for it.[50]

For the prospective clergyperson, the question of spiritual maturity goes to the very heart of the question "When?". The sort of questions to ask of the self are, "When should I submit myself to the formal process of discernment and selection?" Or "Am I sufficiently and robustly mature in Christ to submit myself to that process?" A large and important indicator of spiritual maturity is the extent to which the candidate expresses a willingness to submit to the decision-making process, and to the prerogative of the church, in respect to

---

50   Sarah Bachelard, 'Spiritual maturity and ministerial obligation', in Tom Frame (Ed), *Called to minister: vocational discernment in the contemporary church* (Canberra: Barton, 2009), p, 139.

the question of vocation, most tellingly including acceptance that the church may say "no". Whilst disappointment is a natural response if the church does say no, a refusal or inability to hear that no, or to apportion blame or defect of some nature upon those speaking that no, is a sure sign of spiritual immaturity and, correspondingly therefore, of unsuitability for ordination.

Dedication and commitment

Setting out what he calls "the promissory character of ministry," Stephen Pickard points to the solemn and public nature of the promises made by candidates in the ordination service as the key distinguishing feature between the clergy and laity.[51] Some of the important questions for the candidate or prospective candidate are, then, "Am I the sort of person who can make and keep a promise?" And, "What do I have to do in order to be able to make such promises?"[52] Eugene Peterson, similarly, in articulating the lifelong nature of ordained ministry as, not a temporary job assignment but a way of life, lived out in community, sees the ordination service as "extracting a vow" from the candidates.[53] This is not to be taken lightly, especially as the giving and keeping of a promise, and the extracting of a vow, in the context of the ordained ministry of the church, is intended to be a lifelong commitment.

In his helpful and practical volume, John Adair states categorically that "the most common characteristic of vocational people is their sense of dedication to their art, craft or profession."[54] He writes:

---

[51] Pickard, *Theological foundations for collaborative ministry* (Farnham, UK: Ashgate, 2009), p. 222.

[52] Pickard, *Theological foundations for collaborative ministry*, p. 223.

[53] *The contemplative pastor: Returning to the art of spiritual direction* (Grand Rapids: Eerdmans, 1989), p. 139.

[54] *How to find your vocation* (Norwich: Canterbury Press, 2000), p. 4.

The eminent founder and conductor of Scottish Opera, Sir Alexander Gibson, was once asked in a press interview about the sources of his philosophy of life. He replied: A quote from Rachmaninov has from time to time reassured me that it is not altogether unhealthy to be obsessed with one subject – perhaps to the exclusion of all other concerns and aspects of life: *I am myself only in music, Music is enough for a whole lifetime – But a lifetime is not enough for music.*[55]

It is not surprising, then, that "dedication" is a word with religious overtones, being derived from the Latin *dedicare* meaning "to devote" and "to consecrate". The *Oxford English Dictionary* defines "dedication" as "being dedicated or committed to a task or purpose".[56]

A sense of vocational dedication or commitment, is often accompanied by a conviction that it is not being undertaken exclusively, or primarily, or even at all, for monetary gain, although the biblical principle that "those who proclaim the gospel should get their living by the gospel" (1 Corinthians 9.14) is present in the notion of the stipend or "living" paid to the ordained minister to ensure they are able to carry out their duties free from want for the necessities of life. Whilst there is a sacrificial or self-giving aspect present in a dedication and a commitment to ordained ministry, as there is in many professions and especially the "helping" professions, it does not follow that this is all consuming, nor comes at the cost of the minister's own personal self, relationships or wellbeing. Nonetheless, it is the case that there is some measure of self-giving and self-sacrifice inherent in the vocation to ordained ministry, following the exemplar of Christ:

> Paul understood the ministry as an extension of Christ's death and resurrection. It therefore entails a daily dying to those qualities

---

55 Ibid, p. 4.
56 *Oxford Dictionary of English* (Oxford: Oxford University Press, 3rd edn, 2010).

coveted by most of our culture and a daily rising to Christ's astonishing presence among us.[57]

The qualities of dedication and commitment, or as Eugene Peterson puts it "the extracting of a vow," do demand and require, and will demand and require in an ongoing way, both a determination and resilience that must be sustained over the course of a lifelong vocation, in which "resilience becomes a lifelong journey, underpinning and supporting the whole of our understanding of what vocation is about."[58] In many ways this is the fundamental and essential quality needed in any person who believes they are called into the ordained ministry, in addition to the call itself.

Others orientated

A life of service entails a life orientated toward others. It is not at the exclusion or detriment of the self, for a life of service to others demands times of spiritual withdrawal, retreat and nourishment, following the example of Jesus. (Mark 1.35) Whilst there are, and have been for many generations in the past, disciples called to a life of solitude and seclusion, either alone or with others, to energise the coming of the kingdom of God through sustained prayer, work, or study of the scriptures; for most, much of ordained ministry as with much of life, will be spent with others, both in service and ministry to others, and in the receiving of the same from others.

Central to ministry is the building up of the relationships, the quality of incidental encounters, the time spent in praying for people, the care

---

57 Richard Lischer, 'The called life: An essay on the pastoral vocation,' *Interpretation* 59 (2005), p. 172.
58 Magdalen Smith, *Steel angels: the personal qualities of a priest* (London: SPCK, 2014), p. 8.

given in walking with people through difficult circumstances and the witness that all of this is connected to the love of God known through Jesus Christ. Such things are hard to quantify, and often the outcomes of such encounters are not obvious in the short term, and may never be recognized this side of heaven.[59]

The needs and the demands can, and often are, many and tiring, even overwhelming. At times it may seem a thankless task, in which the gratitude of, or even the acknowledgement of, others, is absent. Resilience is, again, critical. Reflecting on the twelve years he spent as vicar of a West Yorkshire parish, Richard Giles offers this advice, "I often think the Church should make part of basic training for all ordinands a spell among the moors and mills, where 'not impressed' is the most common verdict on practically everything."[60]

Notwithstanding and despite this, it is important also to recognise that one of the many aspects to a life of ministry to and with others is a recognition that it is a life of both giving and receiving. It is important for an ordained minister to be open to receiving the ministry of others. Christopher Cocksworth and Rosalind Brown explain:

> The ordained life begins as it is meant to go on, but it can become increasingly difficult to lay ourselves open to the ministry of others, and especially from members of our own congregations. It can feel like an admission of failure for some to know, or see, that we are being ministered to by others – the very people we have been charged to serve. In fact, it is evidence of success.[61]

---

59 Emma Percy, *What clergy do: especially when it looks like nothing* (London: SPCK, 2014), p. 20.

60 *Here I Am: reflections on the ordained life* (Norwich: The Canterbury Press, 2006), p. 16.

61 *Being a priest today: exploring priestly identity* (Norwich: The Canterbury Press, 2006), p. 55.

Life with others entails listening to them, something we may not always be as good or proficient at as talking, especially those who spend a lot of their time preaching and teaching! This can be especially important in the delivery of pastoral ministry to others, where the urge to fill a space with words, and to reach for solutions, can be irresistible, but often unhelpful. Dietrich Bonhoeffer presciently maintained that "the first service that one owes to others in the fellowship consists of listening to them."[62] Yet, as Bonhoeffer went on to observe, many people looking for someone to listen to them do not find it in the Christian church, chiefly because too many Christians are talking when they should be listening.[63] The other orientated life is one in which the first inclination, especially in pastoral ministry settings, is to listen.

As Martin Percy sums this up, "vital to the flourishing of the community of learning and the individual in formation" are "the profound spiritual exercises" of "being open to God, paying attention to others, and deep listening."[64]

Humility

However gifted one might feel, or appear, a call to ministry is, as we have seen, first and foremost, a call to service.[65] Bonhoeffer maintained that pastoral authority can be attained only by the servant of Jesus who seeks no power of their own, but who sees themselves as equal among others submitted to the authority of Jesus.[66]

---

62   *Life together* (London: SCM, 1954), p. 75.
63   *Life together*, p. 75.
64   'Sacred sagacity: formation and training of ministry in a Church of England seminary,' *Anglican Theological Review* 90 (2008), p. 296.
65   Badcock, *The way of life*, p. 93.
66   *Life together*, p. 85.

This reminds us that service is the opposite of power, and that the gifts of God are never given for the aggrandization and enrichment of the self, but for the benefit of others. This is unsurprising, for the very essence of ministry has its locus in the biblical concept of *diakonia*, a word that has a wide semantic circle of meaning, much of it clustering around the notion of service and especially of service to others. Even the one in the church who literally has all the power and all the authority the world, and even the universe, can possess (Matthew 28.18) came, not to be served, but to serve, and to give his life as a ransom for all (Matthew 20.28).

Theologically, humility is a fundamental criterion to the ordained minister, for the ministry the ordained leader has, and exercises, is always conducted on behalf of another, Jesus the great high priest.

> A desire to place self, rather than Christ, at the centre of the stage is the one quality that cannot be tolerated, as it will transgress this central Christian conviction about the Church – that Christ is the true High Priest; he is the only true Leader.[67]

Further, an awareness of our own dependence on God, and of human sin and mortality, reminds us that, whatever gifts we may receive and exercise, and whatever positions of influence and seeming power and authority we may occupy, these treasures always exist within the clay jars of our own humanity.

> Therefore, since it is by God's mercy that we are engaged in this ministry, we do not lose heart. We have renounced the shameful things that one hides; we refuse to practise cunning or to falsify God's word; but by the open statement of the truth we commend ourselves to the conscience of everyone in the sight of God. And even if our gospel is

---

67 Graham Tomlin, *The widening circle: priesthood as God's way of blessing the world* (London: SPCK, 2014), p. 146.

veiled, it is veiled to those who are perishing. In their case the god of this world has blinded the minds of the unbelievers, to keep them from seeing the light of the gospel of the glory of Christ, who is the image of God. For we do not proclaim ourselves; we proclaim Jesus Christ as Lord and ourselves as your slaves for Jesus' sake. For it is the God who said, 'Let light shine out of darkness', who has shone in our hearts to give the light of the knowledge of the glory of God in the face of Jesus Christ. But we have this treasure in clay jars, so that it may be made clear that this extraordinary power belongs to God and does not come from us. (2 Corinthians 4.1–7)

Human fragility entails acceptance of the possibility of failure. Peter was a failure, and felt a failure. After the crucifixion of Jesus, and after the shame of his betrayal, not once but three times, Peter had returned to his former occupation as a fisherman, where the resurrected Jesus found and restored him on the shores of the Sea of Galilee (John 21.1–19), the very site of Peter's original calling. There will be times of disappointment and failure in the pursuit of any vocation, and so it follows, there will be times of failure for those called to a vocation in ordained ministry. For good reason, then, the very first principle for maintaining a faithful witness in ordained ministry articulated by John Pritchard, in his *Life and work of a priest*, is to not fear apparent failure.[68]

Failure, and the fear of failure, give rise to a sense of vulnerability, that can be both a positive and a negative, depending on how we may respond to it at a given point in time. A robust humility will be needed to turn, over time, what may be perceived as a negative, into a positive, a weakness into a strength, and a perceived failure into a triumph.

---

68 *The life and work of a priest* (London: SPCK, 2007), p. 152.

Prayer

The lifelong vocation of ordination is sustained, and can only be sustained, by remaining in relationship with God, the one who called us into it in the first place. And one of the primary ways that relationship is nurtured, fostered and given expression, is in prayer. Because the ordained ministry is a vocation, not just an occupation, "prayer is not merely a functional means to secure the resources we need to do the work. It is life-changing. We should not pray if we are not willing to be transformed... Even if we can only see with hindsight, transformation does happen when we pray faithfully. The daily rhythm of prayer promotes growth that is imperceptible to the self but evident to others."[69]

Present for good reason then, is this directive contained in the preface ('Concerning the service of the Church') to the 1662 *Book of Common Prayer*:

> And all Priests and Deacons are to say daily the Morning and Evening Prayer either privately or openly, not being let by sickness, or some other urgent cause.

In the Church of England the saying of morning and evening prayer as stipulated by the Prayer Book is also enshrined in canon law, which places an obligation on every bishop, priest and deacon to say daily morning and evening prayer, either privately or openly, and also to celebrate or to be present at Holy Communion on all Sundays and other principal feast days.[70] Many aspirants and prospective candidates for ordination enthusiastically endorse this directive and claim to inhabit it. But it is not an easy or frivolous calling. This is a lifelong commitment that will, at times, be a hard, often an arduous, task, requiring an act of willpower. Richard Giles writes:

---

69 Cocksworth & Brown, *Being a priest today*, p. 107.
70 Mark Hill, *Ecclesiastical law* (Oxford University Press, 4th edn, 2018), p. 104.

One of the treasures of our Anglican tradition is the discipline of the Daily Office. Morning and Evening prayer, said with a sprinkling of colleagues and fellow-workers or (if necessary) alone, ensures that we are rooted and grounded simultaneously in the psalms beloved of our Lord, the scriptures, and the ancient tradition of our Church. In reciting the Daily Office we grow into a sense of unity with all our brothers and sisters across the world who, as the planet spins, with us maintain an unceasing hymn or praise and devotion to God. To remain faithful in the discipline of the Daily Office demands of us, not so much a dance of exaltation, as a steady plod of utter determination.[71]

A determination to prioritise prayer, to persist in prayer, and to foster and nourish a life of daily prayer is, therefore, an essential quality in any candidate for ordination. For good reasons, one of the very first questions asked of any respective candidate will be something like, "please describe your prayer life?". It is a question that should be asked again and again, both by the self of the self, and by others.

Almost all the studies I have seen on the personal wellbeing of clergy and about longevity and resilience in ordained ministry, together with studies on preventing exhaustion and burnout, consistently point to the fundamental importance of a disciplined pattern of prayer. Discipline is important here, because the needs and the tasks will always be there, and the times at which they may appear to be urgent will be many. Of course, there may be occasions on which the right response to a pastoral urgency is to drop everything and respond. But those times will normally be exceptional and rare. The norm will be a regular pattern of prayer, ideally daily, and at a set time. The temptation to not pray today, considering whatever today's particular urgency or pressing tasks may be, will always be

---

71   Giles, *Here I am*, p. 2.

present but should be resisted. The cost is too high. For when the spiritual energy generated by prayer, by spending time in silence with God, and by reflecting prayerfully on the Scriptures diminishes, so too, ultimately, does that which sustains a vocation.

In parish ministry I personally found the discipline of the BCP to be a helpful guide. I advertised the time I would be in the chapel to say morning prayer publicly, and was often joined by parishioners, as well as any theological student or assistant curate placed in the parish. This kept me disciplined, and I rarely departed from the practice of beginning each day in the chapel with morning prayer, either alone or with others. Because there were times when morning prayer seemed unappealing and difficult, and because it would have been easy to not do it and get straight to the many demands of the day, I found the public undertaking to be present ensured I was there at the appointed hour with prayer book in hand, ready to pray, and to read and reflect on the passages from scripture appointed for that day, on days when I felt eager for it and on days when I did not.

The needful gifts of grace

It is never the case that any disciple of Christ, and therefore no person pursuing a possible call to ordained ministry, is without gifts or giftedness.

> There is one body and one Spirit, just as you were called to the one hope of your calling, one Lord, one faith, one baptism, one God and Father of all, who is above all and through all and in all. But each of us was given grace according to the measure of Christ's gift. (Ephesians 4.4–7)

The passage cited above from the letter to the Ephesians gives us assurance and certainty that Christ enables each of the baptised to fulfil the ministry given to them by placing within us the needful gifts of grace. These gifts, given by God and implanted by the Holy Spirit, are often known as the *charismata* or as *charisms* (Romans 12.1–6; 1 Corinthians 12.1–11). A "charism" may be present in the form of one or more of the spiritual gifts, or it may reside in a talent, skill or ability. The charism is implanted by God to benefit, not the individual to whom it is given, but others, both those within the Body of Christ and those beyond it, for the purpose of building up the Body of Christ and furthering the mission of Christ in the world.

We can be assured, then, by the Scriptures, that if God calls, God also equips. But that does not mean we become the "finished product" so to speak at the point of experiencing and professing a call. It means, rather, that God gives us what we need at the time we may need it. Sometimes we may not even know that what we need lies within us, because it may appear as a weakness not a strength.

> Therefore, to keep me from being too elated, a thorn was given to me in the flesh, a messenger of Satan to torment me, to keep me from being too elated. Three times I appealed to the Lord about this, that it would leave me, but he said to me, 'My grace is sufficient for you, for power is made perfect in weakness.' So, I will boast all the more gladly of my weaknesses, so that the power of Christ may dwell in me. Therefore I am content with weaknesses, insults, hardships, persecutions, and calamities for the sake of Christ; for whenever I am weak, then I am strong. (2 Corinthians 12.7b–10)

There are two assurances here:
1. That we do not come empty handed to the moment of decision and to the offering of one's self to the service of God and his church, but we each come with charisms implanted by God – gifts, skills, abilities, talents; and

2. That even where we may not feel especially gifted, and even where we may feel inadequate or weak, or out of our depth and unsure of ourselves, God can and does use that too.

This gives us a confidence that arises out of a deep dependence on, and trust in, God. This is the confidence that the one who calls also equips, so that the one who is sent will be able to do what he or she has been sent to do.

I have found this to be true in the living out of my own vocation as a person in ordained ministry. At secondary school, like many adolescents, I was terrified of public speaking. I can well recall purposefully missing the school bus on public speaking day, and spending the day instead in the video game parlours, shopping centres and local McDonalds restaurant of my suburb, to pass the time. When I did offer for ordination and became a theological student in my twenties, I remember that same fear arising each time I was called upon to speak publicly before my peers, as of course, I was from time to time. The prospect of doing homiletics (preaching class) filled me with dread, but there was no avoiding it, for it was a compulsory subject for ordination candidates. I well recall the anxiety, the feelings of inadequacy, of being trapped in pursuit of a calling I was unsuited for, and all the self-doubt and dismay that came with it, as I prepared for the trial of homiletics class and of delivering my first sermon in the college chapel. Even more excruciating, it was going to be filmed, and I would then have the further ordeal of being compelled to watch the recording with my lecturer. Notwithstanding all of this, when the day arrived and I walked to the pulpit and placed my notes on the lectern, and began to speak, I remember being overwhelmed by an unexpected peacefulness, that gave me a sense of both calm and security, that I did belong here in the pulpit, and that I did have a voice that God wanted me to make heard. I don't recall a single word of what I actually said on that day, but I do recall, very clearly, that sense of calm and purpose, and I am convinced that it is, and was, the work and ministry of the Holy Spirit, implanting within that which I needed at that time to fulfil the call of God on my life.

Authenticity

Finally, it is fundamental that, with a call to ordained ministry, comes a call to authenticity. As Paul exhorted the Corinthians, "be imitators of me as I am of Christ" (1 Corinthians 11.1). Another way of putting this, a little more colloquially, is to "practice what you preach". The Prayer Book for New Zealand Aotearoa captures this with precision and poignancy in its service for the ordination of priests, wherein the ordaining bishop tells the ordinands, "you must be prepared to be what you proclaim".

Though it is barely a sentence, the exhortation of Paul to the Corinthians, "be imitators of me, as I am of Christ", is surely one of the most costly and courageous invitations issued by any leader in the canon of Holy Scripture. There is, of course, a very real and necessary element to leadership and supervision that does entail watching, doing and, to some extent, imitating. A good leader, and a good supervisor of others, does demonstrate and model effective ministry for those in training positions under their supervision. For one assistant with whom I worked, I was only too happy to go over a matter of liturgical necessity several times, until he got it right and was comfortable and confident with that particular task. For another, I only had to observe her conducting a baptism once. Even from my view in the rear pew I could see her poise and self-assurance. She was probably doing it better than me. However, Paul's words here are, in my reading, not really about training and supervising others, nor are they about the Corinthians watching and observing so that they may learn by observing and then doing. I think it is much more personal and intimate than that, and the key is the second part of the sentence, "as I am of Christ". This is an appeal directly to Paul's own Christ-likeness, something only one completely convinced of their own discipleship and integrity in it would dare to proclaim.

Authenticity in ordained ministry resides in personal holiness. That should not surprise, given the presence of the word "holy" in the term Holy Orders, which is frequently used of Anglican ordination. Thomas Dozeman sees the calling to holiness of life and practice as both essential and all-encompassing, in understanding that "the primary responsibility of the profession of ordination" is a call to "serve the sacred in order to mediate holiness to other humans".[72] There is a cost to holiness. It does not always, even often, come easily and naturally. It requires discipline and dedication, together with an acceptance that we will never (this side of heaven) reach perfection. If it does not arise authentically, out of a deep and sincere commitment to Christ and of love for Christ, it will be both hard to sustain, and will almost certainly be recognised intuitively by others as inauthentic, something that is, at the very least, detrimental to, and very often fatal to, a vocation to ordained ministry.

For these reasons, of all the many and varied aspects of the vocation to ordained ministry, I am convinced, after more than twenty years in Holy Orders, that authenticity is one of the most important of all the qualities required of an ordained minister of the church, and probably the hardest to sustain and live out! Think for a moment of the boldness and profundity of Paul's exhortation to the Corinthians, "be imitators of me, as I am of Christ." And now reflect on how that might be applied to your own life as a person in ministry, and when (all the time?), and to whom, to some select people such as a congregation, my family and intimate friends, others, everyone?

---

[72] *Holiness and ministry: a biblical theology of ordination* (Oxford: Oxford University Press, 2008), p. 122.

4. Becoming – formation for ministry

Discerning a vocation to serve God and God's church, coupled with the desire to enter ordained ministry, involves embarking on a journey of discernment and discovery about being and becoming. Because no candidate ever comes to a selection process in a state of complete readiness, the wise selector, bishop, vocational advisor and examining chaplain, is looking and praying for potential, and asking of the candidate before them, "Is God calling this person into Holy Orders?" And, "What can God do with this person, and who might they become?"

One of the considerations in any selection process, in addition to the core questions of call and vocation, will inevitably concern the potential and capacity for the candidate to learn the requisite academic knowledge and acquire the ministry skills to perform the role of an ordained minister. For the selectors, the question may be framed around a consideration of the candidate's present theological understanding, together with their potential to complete a course of academic study in theology.

For many candidates today the journey may begin by entering a theological college, school or seminary, of their own volition, rather than waiting to be selected or sponsored to do so through a formal selection process. In the minds of many of those considering a possible call to ordained ministry, enrolling in a course offered by a theological college is a natural first step, to see and experience what studying theology is like and whether it is for "me".

Notwithstanding this, it is only relatively recently, alongside the parallel development of the concept of a profession in other disciplines, that it has come to be understood as essential for Anglican clergy to be formally trained for their role as ordained ministers of the church. Whilst theological colleges and seminaries have certainly existed for a very long time, it was often considered by those with authority to ordain (in the Anglican Church: bishops) that a decent education in a discipline such as the classics, the arts or law was sufficient in itself, and that the rest could be learned and acquired "on the job" as it were.[73]

Today, the reality is that most bishops and dioceses in the Anglican Church will expect, and often require, an academic award in theology from a recognised institution at tertiary (university) level, as a prerequisite or co-requisite to ordination. For some the standard will be nothing less than an undergraduate or postgraduate degree requiring the equivalent of three to four years full-time study, including mandated subjects in a variety of disciplines.

Preparation

Those who are called, need to be prepared for that to which they are called. In the modern context, in light of the recent professionalisation of the ordained ministry across most Christian churches and denominations, this will entail the acquisition of intellectual and academic knowledge, and the requisite practical skills, as would be the case for most, if not all, professions. It would be incongruous, for instance, to meet a doctor who had only a rudimentary and passing knowledge of medicine and no actual experience of consulting with patients, and who was not formally qualified to practice medicine; just as it would be somewhat alarming for a motor mechanic to

---

[73] Though now quite dated in its conclusions and application, Anthony Russell's *The Clerical Profession* (London: SPCK, 1980) provides a comprehensive account of the gradual professionalisation of Church of England clergy over the course of the nineteenth century in particular.

have never been formally instructed in how to maintain a vehicle through a vocational course of study supplemented by an apprenticeship.

In the same way, ordained ministers of the church are normatively expected to have received a formal education in biblical studies and theology, and to have acquired proficiencies in the practice of pastoral ministry. It is, rightly, the case that the clergy can reasonably be expected to be "the professionals" in respect of things such as the manner in which the scriptures are to be read, interpreted and explained, and that this will usually entail acquiring an understanding of the original languages in which the Bible was written, together with a proficiency in the principles of biblical interpretation. Such knowledge needs to be taught and learned.

Whilst this is true, and widely accepted, it can never be the case that acquiring intellectual knowledge through a course of academic study is, of itself, all that is needed in order to minister effectively. As Andrew Mayes observes, "the language of training... can betray a pragmatic approach to ministry that is simply skills-based and task-focused," leading to "a functionalist view of ministry which emphasises out of all proportion the competencies needed in order to accomplish tasks successfully and with maximum results and greatest efficiency."[74] This does not mean that training is detrimental or unnecessary, it just means that it should always be considered and understood in the wider context of formation.

> The language of formation... makes us ask what deeper work of God is taking place in the candidate: It encourages us to discern the transformative work of the Spirit in us. It prompts us to move from a stress on *doing* to an awareness of *being*, or at least to hold these two models within a creative dialectical tension.[75]

---

74 Andrew D. Mayes, 'Priestly Formation,' in *Developing faithful ministers: A practical and theological handbook* (eds. Tim Ling & Lesley Bentley; London: SCM, 2012), p. 29.

75 Mayes, 'Priestly Formation,' p. 29.

As Emma Percy puts this in her treatise on clerical life, "clergy are trained, but this is as much about forming a character as about acquiring knowledge."[76] We might sum this up succinctly by saying that formal study in an academic environment, and the application of that intellectual knowledge in the actual practise of ministry, are both essential elements of what we might more broadly understand as formation. Concurrently, as indicated by Emma Percy above, what is really being formed and shaped is godly character. This is because, for the candidate for ordination, theological education is never only about acquiring knowledge. The essence of theology – from the Greek *theos* (God) and *logos* (word or words) – is discourse about God, and God is not a thing to be studied in the abstract, but is to be known and to be known by. The Christian encounter with God is transformative, affecting the whole of the person – body, mind and soul.[77] So, it follows, should it ideally be the case that the provision and experience of theological education and training be similarly holistic. There is simply no substitute for a life lived in, and shaped by, the knowledge of God in the face of Jesus Christ (2 Corinthians 4.6). The accumulation of knowledge, skill and experience does not make a person a minister in God's church.

> A person in holy orders could discharge their tasks diligently and still know nothing of the mind of Christ. They could provide religious services in a technically competent manner but reveal nothing of the coming kingdom of God.[78]

---

76 *What clergy do*, p. 7.
77 Alister E. McGrath, *The renewal of Anglicanism* (London: SPCK, 1993), p. 161.
78 Tom Frame, 'The role of vocational training', in *Called to minister*, p. 124.

Formation

The heart of formation, then, is about being and becoming. It is about who I am in Christ, and who I am becoming as a person of faith and, by extension, who I am becoming as a person in ministry. Formation is by no means restricted to a "class" of Christian, such as authorised lay ministers or the clergy. Formation for ministry is shared-in equally by all the baptised. The process of ministry formation for all the people of God is lifelong, for it is fundamentally about discipleship, residing in the call to follow Christ, which is responded to in differing ways, at different stages of life, by the different members who make up the Body of Christ (1 Corinthians 12.1–26).

The language of formation is present throughout Holy Scripture, and used of the creative act in which God forms both the world (Psalm 90), and the human beings within it (Genesis 2.7).

> For it was you who formed my inward parts;
> you knit me together in my mother's womb.
> I praise you, for I am fearfully and wonderfully made.
> Wonderful are your works;
> that I know very well.
> My frame was not hidden from you,
> when I was being made in secret,
> intricately woven in the depths of the earth.
> Your eyes beheld my unformed substance.
> In your book were written
> all the days that were formed for me,
> when none of them as yet existed. (Psalm 139.13-16)

In the New Testament, formation takes on a Christological meaning, descriptive of the manner in which Christ is being formed in both the individual believer and in the community of faith, the church (Romans

8.29; Galatians 4.19). Formation is, then, fundamentally about Christ being formed in us, and we being formed to be Christ-like.

There are good reasons, then, for applying the language of ministry formation more narrowly also to the holistic experience and process by which a disciple is prepared for, and sustained in, the life of ordained ministry – through academic study, the acquisition of ministry experience and skills in the context of ministry placements, and the development of the spiritual disciplines that will sustain a life of ministry and service to others.

The nature of a vocation to ministry emerges, not so much in what one does, but the manner in which one does it. Hence, it is in the conceptual language of formation that the academic and the practical aspects of ministry training and development, and the intellectual and spiritual aspects of faith and discipleship, come together.

> The intellectual aspect of formation is integrally related to the practical. The ability to see the whole of life through the lens of Christian faith requires a gradually deepening commitment to the practices through which Christianity is lived out in daily life, such as regular prayer and Bible study, the discipline of sabbath, stewardship of money and time, care for the poor, and commitment to sexual purity.[79]

Genuine ministry formation only occurs when there is a genuine openness to the process of formation on the part of the one being formed, and that requires a genuine openness to the work of the Holy Spirit.

> Trainers and trainees are encouraged to believe that the Holy Spirit is able to use men and women in ways that exceed their physical strength, go beyond their intellectual capacity and far surpass what they thought God would bless and conquer.[80]

---

79   David Heywood, *Reimagining ministerial formation* (London: SCM, 2021), p. xiv.
80   Tom Frame, 'The role of vocational training', in *Called to minister*, p. 121.

Andrew Mayes captures this well, by writing, "the language of formation, then, points us to an inner work of the Spirit in which our identity in Christ takes shape. In relation to ministerial formation, it is not only a question of the jobs I do but, rather, of the person I am becoming."[81] The pattern is Christ, the Great Shepherd. As the APBA Ordinal exhorts those to be ordained priest, "Be a pastor after the pattern of Christ the great Shepherd, who lay down his life for the sheep."[82]

Finally, an essential element of formation, and of bringing forth and shaping godly character, is repetition. Just as developing expertise in a skill or craft requires continual practice, so too does developing the craft of ministry. This takes time and requires patience, dedication and determination. It cannot be rushed.[83] It is axiomatic then, and sometimes assumed, occasionally wrongly, that no person should ever consider ordained ministry unless absolutely convinced of the fundamental tenets of the Christian faith, as articulated in the ecumenical creeds of the church,[84] and only after having lived out that faith in the context of Christian community for an extended period of time.[85] Further, in addition to all this, and mindful of the admonition of 1 Timothy 5.22 ("Do not ordain anyone hastily"), any person seeking to offer themselves for the lifelong vocation of ordained ministry should be prepared for a years-long experience of formation before the moment of ordination comes, and further prepared for a lifelong process of formation after it.

---

81 Mayes, 'Priestly formation,' p. 30.
82 APBA, p. 793.
83 S.J. Taylor, 'Crafting ministers,' *Theology* 118 (2015), p. 104.
84 The Apostles' Creed and The Nicene Creed.
85 The *Canon Concerning Holy Orders 2004* provides that a person shall not be ordained deacon unless on good and credible evidence the authorising bishop is satisfied that (amongst other requirements) the person is "an active member of this Church or of a Church in communion with this Church and has been for no less than one year."

Lifelong learning

In times past it might have been thought that it was possible to teach, in the space of the time intervening between selection and ordination, all, or at least most, of the skills an ordained minister would need for the duration of their ministry. If anyone really did hold that view, it has all but disappeared today. Instead, colleges, seminaries and other institutions in which prospective clergy are being trained and formed for ministry will be seeking to deliver at ordination, not the finished product, but a work in progress. As in most, if not all, professions today, the pace of change in society, in the delivery and content of information, and in so many other ways, as well as in the context and practice of ordained ministry itself, demands an attitude toward life learning and constant professional development.

> The purpose of theological education is to provide a platform for serious continuing study, including personal study. An educated person is one who recognises the limits of their knowledge and understanding but knows how to go about acquiring new insights.[86]

The reality is, then, that formation in Christian discipleship is always a lifelong commitment.[87] This is one of the ways in which it is right to understand ordained ministry as being analogous to a profession.

Ministry in the church as well as being a vocation is sufficiently analogous to other professions to be regarded as a profession. The positive meaning of being a professional connotes a specialised

---

86 Tom Frame, *A house divided: the quest for unity within Anglicanism* (Brunswick, Vic.: Acord, 2010), p. 209.
87 Heywood, *Reimagining ministerial formation*, p. 25.

competence, a commitment to excellence, integrity, selfless dedication to serve the community and to holding public trust.[88]

One important way that those who do proceed to ordained ministry can ensure they maintain that competence and that trust, is to engage in a process of lifelong learning through undertaking regular professional development, seeking to refresh and renew skills learned in the past or to acquire new ones, through participation in occasional seminars and webinars, conferences, and formal units of study in a particular area or discipline. The practice of professional development is already well embedded in Anglican ministry, usually commencing in the years immediately after ordination in the form of Post Ordination Training, that brings together all those newly and recently ordained into a structured program for acquiring new experiences and skills, in the context of a mutually supportive environment comprised of new ministers.

In recent years, the Royal Commission into Institutional Responses to Child Sexual Abuse, in Australia, which delivered its final report in December 2017, turned its attention to the context in which ordained clergy across a number of Christian denominations exercised their ministry. Several recommendations were made, both generally to all Christian ministers, and more specifically to Anglican ministry. Key among these was Recommendation 16.5, reproduced below.

> The Anglican Church of Australia should develop and each diocese should implement mandatory national standards to ensure that all people in religious or pastoral ministry (bishops, clergy, religious and lay personnel):
> a) undertake mandatory, regular professional development, compulsory components being professional responsibility and boundaries, ethics in ministry and child safety

---

88 Garth Blake, 'Ministerial duty and professional discipline', in *Called to minister*, p. 176.

b) undertake mandatory professional/pastoral supervision
c) undergo regular performance appraisals.

These recommendations point to the need to shift the culture of the church away from the sometimes isolating and highly autonomous practices of the past, where ordained ministers often worked alone for extended periods of time without review, supervision, or other forms of accountability, and in circumstances whereby it was sometimes assumed that all the necessary learning and impartation of skills to sustain a person in the practice of ministry over a lifetime had been "front-loaded in" as it were during the years spent in the seminary or theological college. There is now an acceptance that the clerical life requires ongoing review, consistent accountability, and regular renewal as the world in which our ministry is exercised – and the unchanging gospel is proclaimed – changes rapidly around us. It is now the case that regular review or appraisal (usually annually), participation in professional supervision, and ongoing professional development, will be an expected and vital part of the experience of ordained ministry into the future. This is consistent with the APBA Ordinal, in which one of the questions asked by the ordaining bishop of those being ordained priest, to which a positive commitment is given, is, "Will you undertake such other studies as will help you in your ministry?"

Ministry alone and ministry with others

A further essential element of a life and vocation in ordained ministry is that of collegiality. This is just an acknowledgement of the fact that, with some rare exceptions such as in the solitary monastic tradition, the Christian life is lived in community with others, for like all humans, we need each other in order to grow and flourish throughout the course of our lives.

The APBA Ordinal anticipates, and requires, that the ordained ministers of the church will exercise their ministry both with and to others, and be willing to receive the ministry of others, as well as take up their place in the life and councils of the church.

> Together with your bishop, priest and people,
> You are to take your place in public worship
> Assist in the administration of the sacraments,
> And play your part in the life and councils of the Church.[89]

Seizing opportunities for collegiality and for the sharing of life and ministry with others is especially important for clergy who are working and ministering alone in a context, whether a parish, a school, agency, workplace or other setting. The reality is that ordained ministry can be a lonely and isolating occupation. Sometimes, the vicar of a parish may be the sole person on the payroll in a particular place and may be called upon to do almost everything. There will often be a high degree of personal autonomy in respect to how one arranges the day and plans commitments. This is especially true of parish clergy, to the extent that it is sometimes said that the single cleric working alone in a parish setting is most closely analogous, in terms of employment, to the self-employed. It is also often the case that in a school, a hospital, an agency or other institution, organisation, or workplace, there may be only a single ordained person on staff.

A representative person

Somewhat paradoxically, in addition to being at times a lonely profession, ordained ministry can also often be a very public one. For the ordained,

---

89   APBA, p. 785.

it can be difficult to distinguish everyday life from life as a clergyperson. This is because the ordained ministers of the church are often, if not always, recognised as such, not just in the community of faith but beyond it.

> As a representative person, the Christian pastoral caregiver is also a public figure, and her work is beyond as well as among the Christian assembly. This is especially true of those called to ordination – not least because they undergo a significant public rite of admission into their orders.[90]

Ever since I was ordained, at the beginning of 2001, I have customarily worn the traditional clerical attire of an ordained minister of the Christian church (a "clergy collar" or "dog collar"). Most of the time I wore black shirts with the white collar, which immediately identified me in most contexts as a priest. These days, I almost always wear the purple shirt of an Anglican bishop, with a prominent (pectoral) cross worn around my neck. Dressed like this, I stand out as an ambassador for Christ in my social world and am frequently recognised as one. This can be both good and ill, but mostly good. It means I am readily visible as an ambassador for Christ wherever I go. Of course, all Christians are always ambassadors for Christ, not just the clergy. But attired like this, I am often (though not necessarily always) easily identifiable in public as a Christian and as a representative person.

When I was a vicar, in an inner suburb of Melbourne, it was often easier to get the tram, which ran right out the front of my church and house, into the city centre, rather than to drive the car in and pay the exorbitant parking fees and deal with the ever-increasing nightmare that was then, and is now, Melbourne's traffic congestion. Those journeys gave me first-hand experience of the eclectic mix of people to be found in the community, and first-rate opportunities to be an ambassador for Christ. It is sometimes

---

90   Stephen Burns, *Pastoral theology for public ministry* (New York: Seabury, 2015), p. 86.

uncomfortable to be so easily identifiable as an ambassador for Christ. On one occasion, a rather boisterous man got on the tram and, seeing me dressed in my black clerical attire, strode through the carriage crying "Father. Father!" Unless his biological father were actually on the tram, I knew that could only mean me. "Father, I need to confess," he said as he dropped into the seat adjacent to me. I tried to explain this was not the time or the place for confession and absolution. He was insistent. "I don't think everyone on the tram wants or needs to hear your confession," I pleaded. In fact, by the way they were looking on and listening in, it seemed many of my fellow travellers did want to hear it! I listened to, and then prayed with, the insistent man, in the enclosed and very public space of the Number 8 tram to Flinders Street!

It is difficult, if not quite impossible, for a training college or seminary to prepare prospective clergy for the lived experience of ordained ministry, and for the sort of everyday incidents that will ensue, like the one on public transport I have described above. Some of this will be grasped in ministry placements along the way, and by speaking to mentors, and receiving the supervision and advice of experienced clergy. But much of what it means to be a representative person, and of the implications of a lifelong vocation that is always present whether "on duty" or not, will need to be learned and acquired in light of the lived experience of ordained ministry. One thing is certain – the aspiring minister must be prepared for this reality, and both willing to accept and receive it, and live it.

PART B
THE ANGLICAN WAY

5. Anglican ordination

In the first part of this book we explored the question of what it means to be called by God into the ordained ministry of the church, and how such a call is discerned; both by the individual and by the church, together with the requisite qualities and characteristics. We saw that the very first question asked of a candidate at the ordination of a new deacon is a question about the surety and conviction of that call:

> Do you believe that you are truly called to this order and ministry of deacons, being moved by the Holy Spirit to serve God and build up his people, according to the will of our Lord Jesus Christ and the order of this Anglican Church of Australia?[91]

Notice that, importantly, the candidate is here asked to give a surety about two things. That they are genuinely called and moved by the Holy Spirit to serve God and build up his people according to the will of our Lord Jesus Christ, *and* that they believe this call is in accordance with the order of the Anglican Church of Australia. In answering "I do believe I am called to this ministry," the candidate, therefore, professes two convictions – one, that they do believe themselves to be truly called by God to ordained ministry, and two, that they are convinced that this vocation is to be lived out in the context of the Anglican Church of Australia.

It is, therefore, axiomatic that any person believing themselves to be

---

91   APBA, p. 786.

called to ordination in the Anglican Church, and who may be considering testing that calling, must possess a thorough understanding of, and be able to clearly articulate, how this Anglican part of the wider family of the people of God understands ordination in the context of its historical and theological traditions, and of its liturgy, polity and practice.

Orders of Ministry

All the baptised are collectively and together the *laos*, that is, the very "people of God". As the ecclesiastical lawyer Mark Hill explains, "in its strict sense, the *laos*, or people of God, embraces all those who have been admitted to the Church through baptism, whether ordained or not."[92] Hence, it follows, that the first, and normative, order of ministry is that of the laypeople (or "laity"), which comprises all the baptised. The term "laity" or "laypeople" has, however, devolved in popular usage over time to become a term used to distinguish between the ordained clergy of the church on the one hand, and the unordained people on the other hand. In his careful study of the emergence of ordination and ordained ministry in the early church, Paul Bradshaw traces the evolution of this distinction, together with the associated emergence of the notion that God had arranged for there to be different orders in the church, of which "the laity" constituted a distinct one, and "the clergy" another.[93] Within the order of the laity, there are those called to specific forms of ministry within the church or on behalf of the church in fulfilment of its mission to the world, who may be authorised in some way for that distinct ministry, typically by conferral of a written authority (or license) from the relevant bishop. These persons are, and remain, laypeople, and therefore are members of the order of laity.[94]

---

92   *Ecclesiastical law*, p. 98.
93   *Rites of ordination: their history and theology* (London: SPCK, 2014), p. 39.
94   See the *Authorised Lay Ministry Canon 1992*.

From the earliest years of the church, there can be traced also the emergence from the order of laity of another order, reflecting the use of the term "ordo" in Roman society of the civic officials and leaders who were distinguished by virtue of the office they held from "the people".[95] This points to the differentiation in the church, in ancient times and continuing today, of the calling out of some persons from within the order of the laity, to a different and distinct "order" comprised of those who, having passed through the rite of entry into that order (ordination), may be collectively called "the clergy" so as to distinguish them from "the laity".

Whether ministry is exercised by members of the laity or the clergy, is immaterial in the economy of God. All ministry has a dignity and importance derived from its source in the call of Jesus, and by its conferral in baptism. Although there often appears to be a hierarchy in the household of God, and although in a very real sense there is, especially in episcopal churches like the Anglican Church; and although there must be a form of hierarchy and authority to ensure the effective functioning of the church; theologically there is no differentiation at all between any form of ministry exercised by any of the baptised, but only a distinction of roles and a diversification of responsibilities.

Holy Orders

The reason words such as "vocation" and "call" are used of the clergy points to the essence of what it means to be ordained and to enter (by and through the rite of ordination) into what is described, frequently in canon law, as "Holy Orders".[96] Those who enter Holy Orders enter a lifelong vocation. This is to be distinguished from an occupation, a job, or a career, that a

---

95 Bradshaw, *Rites of Ordination*, p. 39.
96 For example the title of the canon concerned with ordination in the Anglican Church of Australia is the *Canon Concerning Holy Orders* 2004.

person might perform for a period of time, and from a skill, a trade, or a body of knowledge, or the performance of a service, for which a person might receive an income and earn a living, from time to time. Holy Orders is much deeper than any of this. It entails the shaping and the "ordering" of a person's whole life, not just their professional or working life.

> In essence, while a great diversity of theological exposition exists, a mainstream view consistent with Anglican history would be that ordination places the person ordained "into" the relevant "order," and that participation in that "order" is fixed and immutable for life, irrespective of what kind of appointment or lack of it the person so "ordained" may thereafter hold.[97]

To illustrate this – I recall once being asked, as I remember it for the purposes of life insurance, how many hours a week I worked. One answer to that question, I offered, with a completely straight face, is 24 hours a day, seven days a week! Of course, no person can, or should, "work" such hours. And that is the point. For those called to Holy Orders the question is, to some extent, unable to be answered other than by allocating a nominal figure to satisfy the necessary demands of human resource managers, insurers and accountants, and the like, because it is generally impossible for those who have entered Holy Orders to separate life from work, and work from life. Whilst, of course, there are aspects of my life as an ordained clergyperson that are not concerned with ministry – thankfully there is, as there must be, time for a private life with family and friends, and time for hobbies, pastimes and such pursuits, and time for holidays away to enjoy leave, and so on – yet, it is still true, that even at such times, I never stop being a person in Holy Orders. In my first parish ministry appointment, which was to a commuter town on the outskirts of metropolitan Melbourne

---

97   Colin Buchanan, *Historical Dictionary of Anglicanism* (London: Rowman & Littlefield, 2nd edn, 2015), p. 448.

that retained the country town feel of its past, much fruitful ministry occurred in supermarket aisles, carparks, and at the local football ground, as I encountered members of that community in the course of everyday life. This reflects the reality that, the vocation entered upon ordination is one "that is lived out and lived into for the rest of our lives."[98]

Michael Ramsay (Archbishop of Canterbury 1961-1974), in his renowned *The Christian Priest Today*, first published in 1972, offered this advice to candidates on the eve of their ordination.

> Tomorrow in the Ordination Service the answer of Jesus Christ to a fretting world will once again be proclaimed, and you will receive his commission and power to bring peace to many fretting lives. Many such lives will be healed and made strong by your teaching, your care and your love for them. At the Ordination there will be as in every sacrament the seen and unseen part. You will see the Archbishop who ordains you and the many people who will be there praying for you. You will not see that which gives meaning to it all, and this is the re-enactment of what happened on the first Easter evening. Our Lord will be there, with the words "Peace be unto you, as the Father hath sent me, even so I send you"; and the words "Peace be unto you" go always with the wounds in his hands and his side. In the coming years you will know the wounds more than in the past, and you will also know the peace more than you know it now. And one day many will thank God for all that you will have done to make the wounds and the peace known to them.[99]

The point of some significance to grasp here is that something happens at ordination that changes the way the one ordained sees and experiences

---

98   Cocksworth & Brown, *Being a priest today*, p. 223.
99   *The Christian priest today* (London: SPCK, 1972), p. 87.

the world and others in it, and which, correspondingly, changes the way others see and experience the one ordained. It can't really be explained or described. It just is. And it can't really be understood in all its richness and fullness unless you have actually lived it.

For the newly ordained, having been set apart by the act of ordination in a public way, having hands laid on by the ordaining bishop, and the Holy Spirit invoked, something new and different is added, something that was not there before ordination. It will always be there now, even if it cannot be quantified or explained or described. It will still be there even if the one ordained does not, or at a given time is not, exercising the functions of an ordained minister. The reality is that, the ordained person will never be the same again. They will not any longer be considered a layperson or a member of the laity, for ordination entails a setting apart from among the laity. As the influential Anglican theologian Richard Hooker (1554–1600) put it, "ministerial power is a mark of separation, because it severeth them that have it from other men, and maketh them a special order consecrated unto the service of the Most High."[100] This is because ordained ministry is never only a functional exercise, whereby one performs a task or a role or a job for a period of time, and when that role ceases then returns to who they were previously, unchanged. Even though the ordained will almost certainly, and possibly often, move from role to role, and perform a variety of different tasks and functions, they will never return to who they were prior to ordination at the end of those roles, tasks and/or functions. They will always now be an ordained minister in the church of God, whatever function or task they perform, and even if they are performing no ministry-related function, task or role for periods of time.

This does not make the ordained minister any different from or "better" than any of the baptised who each have their own calling and ministry, but it does confer upon the ordained clergy particular roles and responsibilities

---

100 *Ecclesiastical Polity*, Book 5, 77, 1-3.

in the community of faith which they exercise as a representative person. As theologian Hans Kung points out, "it is important to distinguish between the general power given to each individual Christian and the special authority given to individuals who have a public ministry within the community as a whole."[101] Every Christian, for instance, is called and given the requisite authority to proclaim Christ crucified, but "only pastors with a special calling, or those commissioned by them, have the particular authority to preach in the meetings of the community."[102] Similarly, all Christians are empowered to speak words of forgiveness, but only those with a special calling are empowered to speak words of reconciliation and absolution to the community in meetings of the community, and hence to the individual believer.[103]

To sum this up, ordination is to be entered into with the understanding and foreknowledge that it is both indelible, in that it is not intended to ever be removed, and unrepeatable.[104] Once hands have been laid on, and the rite of ordination validly executed, it is not intended this is ever to be undone, nor can it ever be repeated, even if the person ordained chooses not to exercise or perform the duties of an ordained minister, or does not hold a license to do so for a period of time. Ordination is a question of ontology and fact, whilst performance of the duties of an ordained minister is a question of function and role determined by what license an ordained person does, or does not, hold.

---

101 *The Church* (London: Burns & Oates, 1968), p. 439.
102 *The Church*, p. 439.
103 *The Church*, p. 439.
104 It is, however, possible for an ordained minister of the church to be removed or deposed from the exercise of ordained ministry, either voluntarily for some reason, or involuntarily, usually for some serious breach of church or secular law or failure of duty. Colloquially, this is to be "de-frocked". In the Anglican Church of Australia the *Holy Orders (Removal from Exercise of Ministry) Canon 2017* regulates this.

The threefold order

As we have seen, Anglican ordination places the person ordained within Holy Orders. Anglicans further maintain that there are three such orders. This is because the *Book of Common Prayer 1662* makes the confident claim that "it is evident unto all men diligently reading holy Scripture and ancient Authors, that from the Apostles' time there have been these Orders of Ministers in Christ's Church; Bishops, Priests, and Deacons."[105] Notably, this statement relies on both Scripture *and* Tradition ("ancient Authors") for its validity. It is, further, given expression in the 39 Articles of Religion.

> Article 36. *Of Consecration of Bishops and Ministers*
> The Book of Consecration of Archbishops and Bishops, and Ordering of Priests and Deacons, lately set forth in the time of Edward the Sixth, and confirmed at the same time by authority of Parliament, doth contain all things necessary to such Consecration and Ordering: neither hath it any thing, that of itself is superstitious or ungodly. And therefore whosoever are consecrated or ordered according to the Rites of that Book, since the second year of the forenamed King Edward unto this time, or hereafter shall be consecrated or ordered according to the same Rites; we decree all such to be rightly, orderly, and lawfully consecrated or ordered.

Certainly the Greek terms (*diakonos, presbuteros, episcopos*) for each of the orders identified by the BCP and Article 36 (deacon, priest, bishop) occur in the New Testament, though their use and application are not consistent, suggesting there is not yet a settled hierarchy of leadership other than the apostles themselves. The leaders of the church in the first

---

[105] Kevin Giles traces the development of the threefold order, and its eventual hegemony, in the early centuries of the church. *Patterns of ministry among the first Christians* (CollinsDove, 1989), pp. 27-48.

generation or so after the apostles (often called the "apostolic fathers") do, however, know of the existence of a more settled leadership in which there is an episcopate, or oversight, together with deacons and presbyters. Ignatius of Antioch, who was martyred around 110 AD according to most estimates, wrote to the Smyrnaens, "you must all follow the bishop, as Jesus Christ followed the Father, and follow the presbytery as you would the apostles; respect the deacons as the commandment of God." He went on to advise that only that eucharist held under the bishop's authority is valid, and that it was not permissible to baptize without the bishop's authority, a clear statement about the authority in matters of church governance and leadership of the episcopate (bishops).[106] By the time of Ireneaus (ca. 130–202 AD), there is an order of the priesthood that stands in a line of succession extending back to the apostles.[107] The "threefold order" of bishops, priests and deacons, so confidently proclaimed by the *Book of Common Prayer*, is certainly well settled and in existence by the time the *Apostolic Constitutions* were compiled in the late fourth century AD, largely from pre-existing material that had been circulated in the early church for some time.

> Concerning the ordination of presbyters, I who am loved by the Lord make this constitution for you the bishops: When you ordain a presbyter, O bishop, lay your hand upon his head, in the presence of the presbyters and deacons, and pray...[108]

The three orders are cumulative, in that all enter Holy Orders through the rite of ordination as deacon, whilst some of those ordained deacon (but not necessarily all) may subsequently be ordained priest, and a smaller number of those ordained priest may subsequently be ordained and

---

106 Ignatius, *To the Smyrnaeans* 8.
107 *Against Heresies* 4.26.2-4.
108 *Apostolic Constitutions* 8.16.

consecrated (the Ordinal uses both terms) bishop. The rite for each order is distinct, as each order is distinct theologically, and constitute separate and distinct orders of ministry, and not merely different degrees of the same ministry.[109]

In this connection, it is important to understand, especially for those who profess a vocation to the order of priest, that ordination as priest is a new rite and a new ordination entirely, and is not to be thought of in terms of a "progression" from the order of deacon, to the order of priest. Nor should the subsequent ordination as priest of a person previously ordained as deacon, even where the person concerned had offered and been selected for eventual ordination as priest, be thought of in any way as being "automatic" or "by right". A process of examination, together with an assessment of suitability, will be applied to determine whether a person ordained as a deacon who offers to be considered for ordination as priest, should in fact proceed to be ordained as priest. The normative position in canon law is that a person ordained deacon will not be ordained priest until a period of time has passed.[110] The applicable canon in the Anglican Church of Australia prescribes a period of "not less than nine months".[111]

The Ordinal

The BCP Ordinal (the "Form and Manner of Making, Ordaining, and Consecrating of Bishops, Priests, and Deacons according to the Order of The Church of England") included in, and published with, the 1662 *Book*

---

[109] Bradshaw, *Rites of ordination*, p. 165. Bradshaw traces in detail, with constant reference to the "ancient authors," the historical and theological development of rites of ordination, and of the ordained ministry and office itself, across the early centuries of Christianity. *Rites of ordination*, pp. 17-38.

[110] One year in the Church of England (Canon C 7).

[111] *Canon Concerning Holy Orders 2004* s 6(1)(b).

of Common Prayer,[112] sets out the formal requirements for ordination, and remains the authoritative source of these, and other matters of church doctrine and polity, in the Anglican Church of Australia. As Stephen Cottrell notes, the form of the Ordinal used to the present day in both the Church of England and the Anglican Church of Australia is a direct descendent of the very first Ordinal composed by Thomas Cranmer in 1550.[113]

In the preface to the Ordinal, which makes the confident assertion concerning the threefold order of bishops, priests and deacons referred to above, the fundamental requirements for entering Holy Orders are set out. These remain as critical and authoritative today as they did in 1662.

Firstly, there is a stipulation around calling, suitability and examination.

> No man might presume to execute any of them [the offices of bishop, priest or deacon] except he were first called, tried, examined, and known to have such qualities as are requisite of the same.

This equates, broadly, to what we might describe as a selection process today, entailing as it does, validation by representatives of the wider church of the subjective or interior call, a process whereby the candidate is tested and examined, together with an enquiry into the extent to which the candidate displays the requisite personal character and qualities. The significance of this is further elaborated on by the stipulation that the bishop ought not proceed to the laying on of hands without being, either through direct personal knowledge or by the aegis of "sufficient testimony", satisfied of the candidate's "virtuous conversation"; and, further, only "after examining and trial finding him [the candidate] to

---

112 The Ordinal was first published in 1550 and revised in 1552, 1559 and then again in 1662. It is not strictly part of the *Book of Common Prayer* but is usually published with it. G.R. Evans & J. Robert Wright, *The Anglican tradition: A handbook of sources* (London: SPCK, 1991), p. 251.

113 *On priesthood: servants, shepherds, messengers, sentinels and stewards* (London: Hodder & Stoughton, 2020), p. 20.

possess the qualifications required by law", and being satisfied that the candidate has been "sufficiently instructed in Holy Scripture". The latter provision points to the necessity of adequate training and formation prior to ordination.

The moment in the ordination service itself at which the candidate's training, formation and suitability is solemnly testified to, and given public expression, is the presentation. Traditionally the Archdeacon, but in modern rites such as that in APBA another senior cleric who may be joined by others including laypersons and examining chaplains, present the candidates to the ordaining bishop, saying "Bishop in the Church of God, we present to you these persons to be ordained."[114] Norman Doe explains the significance of this moment:

> At the presentation… candidates are presented to the bishop who presents them to the people. The rite involves no obvious spiritual activity in itself: it is not an action of God (except God continues to call the candidate). Rather the liturgy recounts prior events with a pneumatic element: vocation, selection, training. These are fundamental to the vitality of ordination.[115]

Secondly, there is provision for "publick Prayer, with Imposition of Hands".

This is the ordination itself, noting that it is a public event that takes place in the presence of the people of God. The form of the liturgy is critical also, for no person can be "accounted or taken to be a lawful Bishop, Priest, or Deacon" unless "admitted thereunto according to the Form hereafter following". The Ordinal anticipates that the call to ordained ministry is a call to ministry in and with a community, expressed in the context of a

---

114 APBA, p. 784.

115 'Ordination, Canon Law and Pneumatology: Validity in Anglican-Roman Catholic Dialogue', *Ecclesiastical Law Journal* 8 (2006), p. 412.

congregation. Hence the bishop solemnly exhorts a newly ordained priest, just after the laying on of hands:

> Take thou authority to preach the Word of God, and to minister the holy Sacraments in the Congregation where thou shalt be lawfully appointed thereunto.

This reflects the truism that ministry is almost always contextual in the sense that "the call will almost certainly always be geared to some situation or group of people, or even to some place."[116]

Thirdly, there is a necessary conferral of "lawful authority" to give effect to the ordination.

The different patterns of ministry discernible in the New Testament crystallize in the apostolic era in the development of ordination by the bishop.[117] Ordination remains an episcopal function in the Anglican Church, in that the laying on of hands must be performed by a bishop using the prescribed liturgy for the ordination to be "lawful". Ordination itself does not confer authority to carry out the function and role of an ordained minister of the church but must be accompanied by an authorisation from the bishop to perform the functions of the office into which one is ordained in that bishop's diocese. This is usually provided in the form of a license. For these reasons, the newly ordained person is given, even as they rise from the laying on of the bishop's hands, both the "letters of orders" which are documentary testimony to the validity of the ordination that has just taken place, and the license, which is the bishop's written authority to perform the functions of the office into which the candidate has just been ordained in a specific place or context.

---

116 Badcock, *The way of life*, p. 95.

117 Frank Hawkins understands this to be natural culmination of the leadership trajectory of the New Testament. 'The tradition of ordination in the second century to the time of Hippolytus,' in Jones C, Wainwright G & Yarnold E (Eds), *The study of liturgy* (SPCK 1978), p. 298.

Article 23. *Of Ministering in the Congregation*
It is not lawful for any man to take upon him the office of public preaching, or ministering the Sacraments in the Congregation, before he be lawfully called, and sent to execute the same. And those we ought to judge lawfully called and sent, which be chosen and called to this work by men who have public authority given unto them in the Congregation, to call and send Ministers into the Lord's vineyard.

The letters of orders stays with the person ordained for the rest of their life as the definitive documentary evidence of the fact of their ordination, but the licence comes and goes, for with each new post there is a new licence.[118]

Whilst the BCP Ordinal remains foundational, the Ordinal most commonly, if not universally, now in use in the Anglican Church of Australia is that included in APBA (pp. 780–809). Charles Sherlock, in his *Australian Anglicans worship*, very helpfully, and clearly, outlines the process of revision of the BCP Ordinal and the Ordinal contained in the 1978 *An Australian Prayer Book*, in respect to the production of the eventual text of the APBA Ordinal, together with the main theological, liturgical and historical issues encountered by, and engaged with, by the compilers.[119]

Canon law

The body of canon law (or "church law") that the Church of England inherited and subsequently transmitted around ordination forms part of the extensive body of law gathered together in the "Canons of 1603".[120] These canons in turn informed much of the canon law of the Anglican Church of Australia, and continue to have a significant influence in Australia and

---

118 Cottrell, *On priesthood*, p. 28.
119 *Australian Anglicans worship*, pp. 398-417.
120 Sometimes referred as the Canons of 1604 or of 1603/1604.

around the Anglican Communion. The Canons of 1603 have their own long pre-history, extending all the way back to the emergence of what would later become canon law in the early church, and in the ecumenical councils of the undivided church of Christian antiquity. The body of canon law that emerged in the early church in respect to ordination is vast, having its roots in the earliest developments, and its source firmly in the writings of the New Testament and especially the letters of Paul.[121]

In respect to ordination, the Church of England consciously, in various places, links its ritual and practice specifically "to the ancient custom of the church".[122] This same body of church law and "ancient custom" continues to inform the canons and other legal instruments of the Anglican Church of Australia. It is given its current form and expression, in respect to ordination, in the General Synod (of the Anglican Church of Australia) *Canon Concerning Holy Orders 2004*.

The Canons of 1603 stipulate the respective "Quality of such as are to be made Ministers."[123] There is an age requirement – deacons must have attained the age of 23, and priests 24. Consistent with the Ordinal, all candidates must also have attained a degree in, or demonstrate proficiency in, scripture and theology, and provide evidence ("letters testimonial") of their godly life and character. This is consistent with the canon law of the Roman Catholic Church, which requires that, "only those are to be promoted to orders who, in the prudent judgment of their own bishop or of the competent major superior, all things considered, have integral faith, are moved by the right intention, have the requisite knowledge, possess a good reputation, and are endowed with integral morals and proven virtues

---

121   Doe & Ombres, 'The ministry of clergy in Anglican and Roman Catholic canon law,' in *The formation and ordination of clergy in Anglican and Roman Catholic canon law* (Cardiff: The Centre for Law and Religion, 2017), p. 6.

122   Doe, 'Ordination, canon law and pneumatology', p. 410.

123   Canon 34.

and the other physical and psychic qualities in keeping with the order to be received."[124]

Building on the foundation of the Canons of 1603, the *Canon Concerning Holy Orders 2004* sets out the minimum requirements for ordination as deacon in the Anglican Church of Australia. It is very important for prospective candidates for ordination in the Anglican Church of Australia to understand that the provisions set out in canon law are binding on the church and its leaders, and are not to be thought of or regarded as negotiable or flexible.

In part, the *Canon Concerning Holy Orders 2004* requires that:

> A person shall not be ordained deacon unless on good and credible evidence the authorising bishop is satisfied that the person –
> (a) has been baptised; and
> (b) is a confirmed communicant member of this Church or has
>   (i) been received into this Church under the Reception Canon 1981 or any other law of this Church providing for the reception of persons into this Church; or
>   (ii) been received into a Church in communion with this Church under a law of that Church corresponding to the Reception Canon 1981 or a law of that Church providing for the reception of persons into that Church; and
> (c) has a firm conviction of a calling by God to minister in Holy Orders as a deacon; and
> (d) is of good character, as testified by a person specified by the authorising bishop; and
> (e) is an active member of this Church or of a Church in communion with this Church and has been for no less than one year; and
> (f) has completed appropriate training in theological and ministerial formation; and

---

[124] The Roman Catholic *Code of Canon Law 1983* (Canon 1029).

(g) has a sufficient knowledge of Holy Scripture; and
(h) has a sufficient knowledge of and accepts the doctrine, discipline and principles of worship of this Church; and
(i) has a sufficient knowledge of the forms of worship of this Church; and
(j) has demonstrated the physical and mental capacity to minister.

The same canon (in clause 9) further stipulates that "nothing requires that a deacon be at some time ordained priest, the office of deacon being recognised by this Church as a full and distinctive order within the historic ministry of this Church."

Prior to ordination as deacon, priest or bishop, the candidate for ordination will also make an oath or affirmation of canonical obedience in accordance with the *Oaths Affirmations Declarations and Assents Canon 1992*. It is, therefore, fundamental that any person considering or seeking ordination in the Anglican Church of Australia is both aware of the content of this, and able and willing to make it, should the time for doing so come.

The Oath or Affirmation of Canonical Obedience.

> "I .... do swear that I will pay true and canonical obedience to .... [the bishop of the diocese or where applicable the bishop of the diocese sponsoring an ordination] and the successors of that bishop in all things lawful and honest. So help me God!"

The nature and content of this oath is reflected also in the Ordinal, wherein the candidate for ordination is asked, "Will you reverently obey your Ordinary, and other chief Ministers of the Church, and them to whom the charge and government over you is committed, following with a glad mind and will their godly admonitions?" The reply expected is, "I will endeavour myself, the Lord being my helper." In the APBA rite, the question asked of those to be ordained deacon is, "Will you accept the order and discipline of the Anglican Church of Australia, submitting yourself to the lawful authority of your bishop and others set over you in the Church?" to which the ordinand replies "I will, by God's grace."

In addition to the oath or affirmation of canonical obedience, the *Oaths Affirmations Declarations and Assents Canon 1992* requires that two further declarations be made prior to ordination.

The declaration and assent to doctrine and formularies:

"I...................... firmly and sincerely believe the Catholic Faith and I give my assent to the doctrine of The Anglican Church of Australia as expressed in the Book of Common Prayer and the Ordering of Bishops, Priests and Deacons and the Articles of Religion, as acknowledged in section 4 of the Constitution, and I believe that doctrine to be agreeable to the word of God.

I declare my assent to the Fundamental Declarations of The Anglican Church of Australia as set out in sections 1, 2 and 3 of the Constitution.

In public prayer and administration of the sacraments I will use the form prescribed in the Book of Common Prayer or a form authorised by lawful authority and none other."

And the Assent to Constitutions and Laws:

"I .... do solemnly and sincerely declare my assent to be bound by the Constitution of the Anglican Church of Australia and the Constitution of the province of............. and of this diocese and by the canons, statutes, ordinances and rules, however described, from time to time of the synod of this diocese and of the General Synod and the provincial synod (or council) which have force in this diocese."

These are serious and solemn declarations that require careful and considered reflection. It follows that, in preparing to make such declarations, and in considering whether they are able and willing to do so, any prospective candidate for ordination should be very clear about the content and the implications of what is meant by:

- the belief and practice of the Catholic faith,

- the doctrine of the Book of Common Prayer and the Articles of Religion,

- the Fundamental Declarations of The Anglican Church of Australia.

Further, the ramifications of agreeing to use in public worship the *Book of Common Prayer* or another lawfully authorised form of liturgy and none other, should also be known and understood; together with what is entailed by agreeing to be bound by the Constitution of the Anglican Church of Australia, together with the canons, statutes, ordinances and rules in force in their diocese.

These matters are further explained and elaborated in a later section of this book: 7. Anglican belief and practice. The content of the canons that have been referred to is fully set out in the appendices.

Function and Ontology

The canons of 1603 require that no person be ordained deacon in the church unless that person had "title" to a ministry appointment. In this context, "title" means a geographical or physical location in which to serve a community of persons.[125] This reflects the longstanding tradition of the

---

125 The requirement that no one is to be ordained "without a title" was formalised in Canon 6 of the Council of Chalecdon, held in 451 AD.

church that ordained ministry is always lived out in the context of service with and to a community.

> It hath been long since provided by many Decrees of the ancient Fathers, that none should be admitted either Deacon or Priest, who had not first some certain Place where he might use his Function. [126]

This continues to be the case in most parts of the Anglican Church of Australia today, in that ordination will only proceed in circumstances whereby the candidate has first been nominated to a ministry position to which the candidate can be licensed after ordination. In other words, there must be a place or community in which the newly ordained person can exercise their ministry, in order for ordination to proceed. This brings together the notions of being and doing, or more technically, ontology and function. Importantly, this does not mean that Anglican ordination is limited to a particular place and community, whether a congregation, parish or whole diocese, for the Anglican understanding of Holy Orders is that there is a universality to ordination that extends beyond geography, and beyond a particular congregation or community, and beyond even the diocese, province and national church. Having once been validly ordained by a bishop, all that the clergyperson needs in order to exercise a ministry in another place, even another diocese or another part of the worldwide Anglican Communion, will usually be a letter of good standing from the current bishop, and the requisite authority in the form of the license from the receiving bishop. There is no re-ordination in the new ministry setting, for the validity of Holy Orders extends beyond the geographical location in which it took place. Rather, the question is one of recognition and of role and licensing.

The practical outworking of these two concepts – of ordination and

---

[126] Canon 33 of the Canons of 1603. For the historical development of this canon – Sarah Coakley, 'Lay and ordained ministry: some theological reflections,' *Sewanee Theological Review* 43 (2000), p. 207.

role, of being and of doing, or of ontology and function – often vests in the question, invariably asked as part of the selection process, as "to what" the person who professes a vocation to Holy Orders believes they are being called by God to do if ultimately ordained. In relation to this, Christopher Cocksworth and Rosalind Brown, somewhat ominously, observe:

> A lot of theological blood has been spilt over whether ordination is about what we do, a set of functions that activate our ordination, or about who we are, a way of being in the life of the Church that is indelibly marked upon us at ordination. More technically, is ordination *functional* or *ontological*?[127]

As complex as this may be theologically, it is relatively straightforward in reality, for, as we have seen, ordination is never a personal or individual thing, and does not exist in and of itself, but is always directly related to a context, most often a community, in which the ordained will exercise their ministry. The World Council of Churches' so-called Lima document (*Baptism, Eucharist and Ministry*, 1982), summed this up well:

> The ordained ministry has no existence apart from the community. Ordained ministers can fulfil their calling only in and for the community.[128]

The essence of the ordained life is the same as that of the Christian life – it is to live in relationship with God, and for that relationship to be expressed and lived out with others. All the baptised are called to this vocation, as all are corporately a "holy priesthood" and a "chosen race" as God's own people.

---

127 *Being a priest today*, p. 5.
128 *Baptism, Eucharist and Ministry* (Geneva: World Council of Churches, 1982), p. 18.

> Come to him, a living stone, though rejected by mortals yet chosen and precious in God's sight, and like living stones, let yourselves be built into a spiritual house, to be a holy priesthood, to offer spiritual sacrifices acceptable to God through Jesus Christ… You are a chosen race, a royal priesthood, a holy nation, God's own people, in order that you may proclaim the mighty acts of him who called you out of darkness into his marvellous light. (1 Peter 2.4-5,9)

It should be noted that, in considering function and practice, the fact of ordination comes first. We first inhabit Holy Orders, exist in it, and let it become part of our being, before we exercise a function. The critical question in the discernment process is not, then, "What will you do in the church?" Or, "What do you believe you are being called to do?" Or, "What would like to do?" But, "Are you being called into Holy Orders?" Notwithstanding this, many candidates for ordination do come with a strong sense of what God is calling them to do, and many come expressing an entirely functional sense of call – "I want to be parish priest" or "a prison chaplain", for instance. In this way, ontology and function almost always, inevitably, come together in the spoken and unspoken profession of the one experiencing a calling, and, correspondingly, for those charged with discerning it.

6. A unique history – Anglicans in Australia

In the not-too-distant past it could have been safely assumed that almost all candidates for ordination in an Anglican diocese would have been baptised and confirmed in the Anglican Church, and only ever attended an Anglican Church. They were lifelong (or "cradle") Anglicans. This was at a time when almost everyone in Australia was at least nominally a member of a Christian church, and when movement between denominations was much less common than today. Those two things have changed dramatically in the space of a few generations in Australia and across much of the western world, with the numbers of persons claiming allegiance to a Christian church declining, and movement between denominations becoming far more common among those who remain. As denominational loyalty diminishes, and movement between the denominations becomes more fluid, it is not surprising that a significant number of people experiencing a vocation to Anglican ordination have come to the Anglican Church from another part of the Christian family, and that many have had several years of experience in other Christian churches before finding a home in Anglicanism.

My own personal experience is testament to this. Having been baptised in a Methodist Church and taken to Sunday school in our local Uniting Church of Australia parish, I attended a Roman Catholic secondary school as a teenager, and in early adulthood found my way back into the life of the Christian church through a Pentecostal community where I met my wife Karen and where we worshipped together for several years. Only after all those divergent experiences did we find our way to an Anglican parish church. When we finally settled into the Anglican tradition and had become assured this was our spiritual home, and were then confirmed, we were well into our twenties.

These changes in religious affiliation, and this fluidity in church attendance is, unsurprisingly, reflected also in candidates for Anglican ordination. In most years, in the Diocese of Melbourne where I work, about half of those being ordained will have come to Anglicanism from another Christian church, and in some years the proportion is higher than that. Many of those I see who are presenting themselves as candidates for ordination are doing so with five years or less experience in an Anglican worshipping community, and some with significantly less than that.

None of this is wrong or especially concerning, and that God continues to send men and women to serve the mission of the church in our Anglican context gives us much to rejoice about. The reality is, however, that it is difficult to discern a vocation to Anglican ordination when one is not really formed in Anglicanism, and where one's spiritual life has not been shaped by it over the course of years. As important as rituals are (and they are), the laying on of hands by the bishop in the rite of confirmation or reception into communicant membership cannot impart what can only be gained and conferred by sustained and active participation – Sunday after Sunday, and week after week – in the life of the church and its liturgies. For good reason does the *Canon Concerning Holy Orders 2004* stipulate that no person can be ordained unless they are "an active member of this Church or of a Church in communion with this Church and has been for no less than one year." That stipulation of one year's membership in the church is a minimum. Ideally there will be several more years of formation, lived out in an Anglican context and community, before a vocation to Holy Orders comes to be discerned.

This is especially important in Anglicanism, which has very few distinct doctrines of its own and in which even the question of whether there is an "Anglican theology" at all is a live one (more on this later). The distinctive feature of Anglicanism, or "the Anglican way", has often been described as comprising those beliefs and practices that arise directly out of its liturgy and in particular the 1662 *Book of Common Prayer*, which remains the authoritative source of belief and practice for Australian Anglicans to the present day. The classical summation of this concept is found in the Latin maxim *lex orandi, lex credenda*, which translates to something resembling "the law of what is prayed is the law of what is to be believed." Apart from the benefit of being formed and shaped in the life and rituals of the church through participation in worship, and through the absorbing of the Prayer Book tradition via participation in its rites, lifelong or cradle Anglicans have much more opportunity to be schooled and educated in the unique and particular history of Anglicanism, together with the manner in which that history and its traditions are reflected in different aspects of Anglican church life and polity.

Whilst there is no substitute to sustained participation in the life of the church in respect to formation, matters of history, doctrine and church polity can be taught and absorbed through reading and reflection. Hence it is important that any person aspiring to Anglican ordination, whatever their background and no matter how long, or how short, a period of time they have been a member of the Anglican church, understands as fully as possible the unique history of the Anglican church in its Australian context, together with its origins in the English church.

Names and titles, and their meaning

It is not uncommon to be asked, often in casual conversation and sometimes among those new to the Anglican church, whether the Anglican Church of Australia has anything much to do with the Church of England? The answer is that the Anglican Church of Australia is in fact the same church, or at least belongs in the same family of churches, as the Church of England.

Up until 1981, when the name was officially changed, the Anglican Church of Australia was, in fact, known as "The Church of England in Australia."[129] This piece of history makes the link pretty plain, and interprets the old story about nominal members of the church becoming frustrated when unable to find the familiar "CofE" on a form asking for their religious affiliation, being unaware that, since 1981, they ought to tick the box marked "Anglican."

The term "Church of England" refers historically to the two ecclesiastical (or church) provinces of Canterbury and York, occupying the land mass of present-day England. This is not synonymous with the United Kingdom, in that Scotland, Wales and Northern Ireland are not included in either province. The origins of what is today called the Church of England extend at least as far back as the mission of Augustine, who was sent by Pope Gregory the Great to establish, or as it turned out to re-establish, Christianity in Britain in 597 AD. A Christian presence in the British Isles goes back much further in time than the mission of Augustine however, and indeed, Augustine himself was surprised (and relieved) to find that Bertha, the wife of Ethelbert the reigning king of the area of his arrival in present day Kent, was already a Christian.

The association of "Anglican" with "Church of England" has its origins in the Latin *Ecclesia Anglicana* which is used in the 1215 Magna Carta, and thereafter increasingly elsewhere, to describe the presence and form of the Christian church in England. At the time of the Magna Carta there was only one Christian church present in England, of which the Pope was the titular head. The term "Anglican" was later applied to the Church of England to distinguish it from the several Christian churches that had emerged from the Reformation of the sixteenth century and is then used extensively thereafter to describe the churches across the world having their origins in, and tracing their historic foundations to, the Church of England, often

---

129 More precisely, the exact title from 1869-1961 was "The Church of England in the dioceses of Australia and Tasmania," and from 1962-1981 "The Church of England in Australia."

through the aegis of missionary activity as the British Empire expanded across the globe. As Richard Giles explains, "Anglican has now come into regular use to describe all or any of the churches across the world that have sprung from the Church of England – originally in areas colonized by the British, and subsequently in other parts of the world where Britons were found to be living and trading."[130]

In some parts of the world, the associations to England were not as palatable as they were in other places. In Australia, as we have seen, the local expression of the Anglican Church came to be simply called "The Church of England in Australia", a title that persisted until 1981. In other places, notably Scotland and the United States of America, the term "episcopal" (meaning "of bishops" and pointing to the fact the church is led by bishops) was used to describe the same church. The result is that the local expression of the Anglican Church in Scotland and the United States of America, and in some other parts of the world, is known to this day as "the episcopal" or "the episcopalian" church. This is not a separate or different expression of the Anglican Church, but a matter of names and titles, in that both the Scottish Episcopal Church and the Episcopal Church in the United States of America are both part of the worldwide Anglican family of churches.

The Anglican Church of Australia, and Australian Anglicans, are, first and foremost, an expression of, and a tradition within, the worldwide Christian religion that extends all the way back in time to its founder, Jesus of Nazareth. Further, the Anglican Church of Australia, and Australian Anglicans, are collectively members of the one global family of Christians within the broader Christian religion, comprised of those churches having historic connections to, and a living relationship with, the Church of England in England. This association of Anglican churches is often spoken of as the worldwide "Anglican communion", the term "communion" meaning a fellowship, association or community. The communion is given

---

130 *How to be an Anglican: A beginner's guide to Anglican life and thought* (Norwich: The Canterbury Press, 2011), p. 4.

titular expression in the office of Archbishop of Canterbury, which has a spiritual and symbolic importance as the figurehead and leader of the worldwide Anglican communion. The bond is one of affection, borne out of a respect for the historic primacy and importance of the office. The Archbishop of Canterbury has no actual authority in any of the worldwide Anglican churches outside of England itself, each of which are fully autonomous. Put another way, there is no office in the Anglican church equivalent to that of the Pope in the Roman Catholic church, and the Archbishop of Canterbury is certainly no "Anglican Pope".

Beginnings in Australia

In light of the history briefly outlined above, it is understandable then that Tom Frame begins his study of Anglicanism in Australia with this observation:

> The Anglican Church of Australia is not a newly created or fashioned stand-alone religious entity. It is descended directly from the Church of England, which has claimed historical continuity with the teaching and mission of Jesus Christ and the undivided Christian Church of apostolic antiquity.[131]

The beginnings of the Anglican Church in Australia extend back in time further even than the foundation of the colony of New South Wales itself. The Anglican priest Richard Johnson was appointed chaplain to the penal colony of New South Wales in England prior to the establishment of the colony and arrived in New South Wales with the first fleet on 26 January 1788.

---

131 *Anglicans in Australia* (Sydney: University of New South Wales Press, 2007), p. 23.

At the first Christian service, at Sydney Cove a week later, on Sunday 3 February 1788, Johnson took as his text Psalm 116:12-13:

> What shall I render unto the Lord
> for all his benefits towards me?
> I will take the cup of salvation,
> and call upon the name of the Lord.

Of course, the land that we now call Australia was not uninhabited when Chaplain Johnson and the first fleet arrived in 1788. There was already, and had been for many centuries, an indigenous culture, rich in history and tradition, and with its own spirituality and theology. The subsequent story of the interaction between the colonisers, with whom the Anglican church arrived, and the indigenous inhabitants of the land, is an often painful and regrettable one, whilst the work of reconciliation remains ongoing and unresolved. One aspect of reconciliation among many others, that is especially important to people of faith, involves a recognition of the unbroken and ancient presence of indigenous Australians in the land, accompanied by a willingness and an openness to hear, and respect, the unique spirituality and theology of indigenous Australians.[132] The opportunities for this will vary across communities and localities, and may need to be sought out by individual candidates in the context of their own diocese, or with the assistance of the National Aboriginal and Torres Strait Islander Anglican Council (NATSIAC).[133]

In the first few years of the life of the fledgling colony of New South Wales the presence of the Anglican Church was embodied by the chaplains, who were accountable to, and under the authority of, the military Governor.

---

[132] A good point of reference in respect to this is the work of Garry Worete Deverell, *Gondwana Theology: A Trawloolway man reflects on Christian Faith* (Morning Star Publishing, 2018).

[133] National Aboriginal and Torres Strait Islander Anglican Council - Home (natsiac.com).

Johnson, who returned to England in 1800, had been joined in 1794 by the Reverend Samuel Marsden, who would remain in the colony until his death in 1838, and would be during that time, a sometimes divisive, and always formidable, figure. In 1823, as the colony of New South Wales grew, and the church with it, the Church of England in Australia was placed under the administrative and ecclesiastic authority of the diocese of Calcutta in India. At this time the first Archdeacon, Thomas Scott, was appointed. When Scott resigned and returned to England in 1828, William Grant Broughton followed him as Archdeacon. A very significant development in the life of the Anglican Church in Australia followed a few years later, when in 1836, at the recommendation of the Governor of New South Wales, Sir Richard Bourke, William Grant Broughton became the first (and only person ever to be so appointed) Bishop of Australia (all of it!).

Broughton had, from the time of his arrival in the colony, embarked on an ambitious and energetic program of church expansion, travelling widely from settlement to settlement, and seeking a constant supply of clergy from England to assist in the organisation of the church and the proclamation of the gospel across Australia. With his appointment as bishop it became possible for the instruments of church life and governance to be consolidated and expanded under local leadership. As a bishop, Broughton could conduct confirmations, ordain clergy, and oversee the creation of parishes and church schools. In 1847 came a further, significant, development, when new dioceses were created in Melbourne, Adelaide, and Newcastle, with Tasmania already in existence as a diocese from 1842. With the discovery of gold, first in Victoria and then in New South Wales, the colonies began to grow rapidly, and the instruments of church governance were not far behind. A geographical system of organisation was established, replicating that of England, with the diocese and the local parish within it as the core units of organisation. The Church of England in Australia was eventually organised into a network of dioceses, today numbering 23, covering the whole of the entire geographical expanse of Australia.

An established church?

The Church of England, in England, has, for many centuries, occupied a place of social, political, and legal importance, as well as religious importance, as the "established church" of that land. This has meant the Church of England (in England) has a particular role and place in the social and political structure of Great Britain, consistent with that of a "state church". This is, often, most clearly seen on occasions such as a royal wedding or funeral, by the status of the British monarch as the "Supreme Governor" of the Church of England, and the presence of Church of England bishops in the British parliament in the House of Lords (the "Lords spiritual"), and in other formal and often ceremonial ways.

It is important to note that, if this was ever true of the Anglican Church in Australia, it was only true in the earliest years of the colonial period, in the sense that it was initially, widely assumed both in England and in New South Wales that the Church of England would be, or would become, the established church of the land.[134] Within a few decades of the establishment of the colony, however, it became increasingly clear that such a claim was untenable and unreflective of the emerging reality. This was due to a mixture of factors, including the strong representation of largely Irish Roman Catholics and Scottish Presbyterians among the growing population, and the progressive outlook of many of the settlers and early leaders of public life, who tended toward favouring the separation of church and state consistent with the Enlightenment principles then widely held across the world. The result of this history is that the Anglican Church in Australia does not today, if it ever did at some point in the distant past, occupy a position in social and public life equivalent to that which the Church of England has in the past, and continues to hold today, in England,

---

134 Keith Rayner. 'The idea of a national church in Australian Anglicanism,' in *Agendas for Australian Anglicanism: essays in honour of Bruce Kaye* (eds. Tom Frame & Geoffrey Treloar: Adelaide: ATF Press, 2006), p. 33.

despite the early hopes and aspirations of Bishop Broughton and others that it would.

Almost from the beginning of the colony, the Anglicans were compelled to recognise that other Christian churches were also active in New South Wales. This was given tangible expression in 1834 when Father John Bede Polding was consecrated as the colony's first Roman Catholic Bishop. Any hopes that the Anglican Church would attain the status of an established or state church in Australia were effectively ended with the passage of the *Church Act* in 1836,[135] the same year Broughton was consecrated the first Anglican Bishop of Australia. The *Church Act* provided state aid for the building of churches, and for the deployment of clergy, to the Roman Catholic and Presbyterian churches that were already present in the colony, as well as the Church of England (the Anglican church), giving a legislative authority to the already evident religious and social pluralism of the colony. As Bruce Kaye categorically describes it, the passage of the Church Act was "a death blow" to any prospect of the Anglicans exercising a monopoly on religion in the colony.[136] The Anglican church in Australia has been, ever since, like the other Christian churches and denominations present in the nation, essentially a voluntary association, largely reliant for its sustenance and survival on its members and supporters, rather than the state.

Increasingly, from the middle of the nineteenth century, the colonial governors and legislatures understood the nature of their society to be both secular and pluralist, and afforded no particular church or religious movement any special status or function in the instruments of society and government. This did not mean the Anglican church was not given privileged or favoured treatment – it often was – but it did mean that

---

135 Properly, *An Act to Promote the Building of Churches and Chapels and to Provide for the Maintenance of Ministers of Religion in New South Wales*. It was signed into law by Governor Bourke on 29 July 1836.

136 *Reinventing Anglicanism: A vision of confidence, community and engagement in Anglican Christianity* (Adelaide: Openbook, 2003), p. 63.

favouritism, or perceived favouritism, was not officially sanctioned by the state, nor ever enshrined in secular law. When the six colonies became states with the foundation of the Commonwealth of Australia in 1901, the principle of religious pluralism was written into the new nation's constitution in section 116, which reads, "The Commonwealth shall not make any law for establishing any religion, or for imposing any religious observance, or for prohibiting the free exercise of any religion, and no religious test shall be required as a qualification for any office or public trust under the Commonwealth."

Towards a National Church

As we have seen, William Grant Broughton was initially appointed in 1836 as bishop of the entire continental land mass of Australia. As the colonies grew, and centres of population emerged, new dioceses were successively created, and bishops installed to lead them. In 1850, Bishop Broughton, now installed as the first Bishop of Sydney and continuing to be the "metropolitan" (or senior) bishop in the Australian church, convened a conference of the six Australasian bishops (this included Bishop Selwyn of New Zealand) in office at the time. The primary purpose of the meeting was to discuss and consider how the Anglican Church in Australia should be structured and governed. By this time it was widely acknowledged that the emerging Australian Church lacked an institutional structure capable of facilitating its growth into the future, and of providing a clear basis for its organisational structure and patterns of church authority and governance. Broughton was especially troubled by the lack of the formal instruments of governance that were bestowed upon the Church of England in England by virtue of it being the established church, but which were, as we have seen, lacking in the Australian context, where it was increasingly clear they did not, or could not, apply.

Some of the proposals put forward at the 1850 conference to introduce formal instruments of governance, and to allow for church convocations, were strongly criticised by the lay members of the church as not providing adequate means for their participation in church affairs. The bishops went back to the drawing board and, in response, developed a proposed form of governance in which the episcopate (the bishops) occupied a distinct role, but in which laypeople were also afforded a significant role and considerable input through the instruments of church assemblies (later synods). The model of governance that ultimately emerged is often described as "episcopally led and synodically governed". Bishop Perry, in Melbourne, who championed such an approach, was the first to establish this in practise with the passage of the Victoria *Church Act* through the colonial legislature in 1854. This enabled the church in the colony of Victoria to convene a synod comprised of the bishop, and representative clergy and laypeople, to make and pass laws for itself and for its own governance, rather than to rely on the civil legislature (the parliament) to make laws for it. In many ways, this model of church governance not only prevailed in Australia, but came to influence Anglican churches around the world.

Because Australian Anglicanism had become dispersed across different dioceses, it began to assume distinctive forms in particular places, inherited from church related factions and controversies at work in England and world Anglicanism, informed also by the nature of the new colonies. The colony of Victoria was separated from New South Wales in 1851, for instance, and developed its own character, and its own legal and political environment. As Bruce Kaye explains:

> In looking at the development of the national church organisation, it is vitally important to realise that for the greater part of the nineteenth century the nation itself did not exist in any sense at all… Even when the nation did come into existence with Federation in 1901, it did so

in a relatively loose form, and it only just managed to include all the current member states.[137]

For the latter half of the nineteenth century, the Anglican Church in Australia existed in the form of individual, autonomous dioceses distributed across the colonies. A move toward a national church structure continued, however, after Bishop Broughton's efforts in the 1850 conference and the years following it, and crystallised during an 1872 conference of clergy and laypeople at which the form of a General (nation-wide) Synod (officially "The General Synod of the Dioceses in Australia and Tasmania") made up of clergy and laypeople representing each of the individual dioceses was established. The General Synod met for the first time over thirteen days in 1872. The ability and effectiveness of the General Synod to both govern and to unify the national church proved, however, to be minimal, largely in light of the resolution made at the time of its foundation in 1872 that decisions and determinations made by the General Synod could only become law in individual dioceses if accepted by the synod of that diocese.[138] Consequently, it continues to be the case to the present day that most canons (laws) affecting the order and good government of the church adopted by the General Synod only have effect in a diocese if subsequently adopted by the synod of that diocese.

Towards a national constitution

Although first proposed as far back as the 1850 church conference, the development, and ultimate adoption, of a national constitution for the Anglican Church in Australia took much longer to resolve. A committee,

---

137 *A church without walls: being Anglican in Australia* (Sydney: Dove, 1995), p. 46.
138 John Davis, *Australian Anglicans and their constitution* (Canberra: Acorn, 1993), p. 46.

delayed by the outbreak of the First World War in 1914, was eventually formed and reported to the General Synod in 1921. A draft constitution was prepared and considered at a constitutional convention held in 1926. The convention resolved to commend its proposals to each diocese, stating the purpose of its work as being "to claim and secure for this daughter Church all rightful freedom and needful fellowship in life and work, that it may the more effectually fulfill its mission and ministry."[139] The synod of the Diocese of Sydney were, however, unable to accept some of the provisions of the draft constitution, and were joined in their opposition to it, and desire for further amendments, by some conservative Anglo-Catholics in other dioceses, prominently the influential vicar of St Peter's Eastern Hill in the Diocese of Melbourne, The Revd Farnham Maynard. Ultimately, as John Davis puts it in his thoroughly researched thesis on the development of the constitution, the initial enthusiasm of the 1920's "ended in stalemate", partly due to the onset of the Great Depression.[140]

Whilst stalemate ensued during the years of the Second World War, by 1950 the tide was turning, and the campaign to achieve a constitution for the Australian church received fresh emphasis when the Archbishop of Canterbury, Geoffrey Fisher, visited Australia and preached the sermon at the commencement of the 1950 session of the General Synod. Fisher, the first Archbishop of Canterbury to visit Australia, proved to be "of great influence" in respect to the push for a constitution.[141] Much of the 1955 meeting of the General Synod was concerned with consideration of a draft constitution that was eventually agreed to. The constitution then had to be considered, and ultimately agreed to, by the synod of each of the individual dioceses, a process that consumed the final years of the 1950s. Finally, both the federal parliament and each of the state parliaments also had to adopt a *Church of England in Australia Constitution Act*. What is now

---

139 Davis, *Australian Anglicans and their constitution*, p. 65.
140 Davis, *Australian Anglicans and their constitution*, p. 78.
141 Davis, *Australian Anglicans and their constitution*, p. 133.

the constitution of the Anglican Church of Australia finally came into effect on 1 January 1962.

At the core of the attempts to develop, and put in place, a national church constitution, was the imperative to not only establish national instruments of church governance and organisation but to secure a sense of an independent and recognisably Australian church as well. The adoption of the constitution represented a large and important step towards the full autonomy of the Anglican Church of Australia from the Church of England, and marked the emergence of a truly independent and separate Anglican Church in Australia, with the power to shape its own affairs – political, legal, and organisational. This crystallised, at least symbolically, in 1966 when a canon was introduced at General Synod to formally change the name of the church from the "Church of England in Australia" to the "Anglican Church of Australia". It took several years for this to be adopted by each of the individual dioceses through their own diocesan synods, but the change of name finally came into effect in 1981.

7. Anglican belief and practice

In his highly readable and engaging little book, *How to be an Anglican*, Richard Giles makes the, at first reading rather startling claim, that the ensuing chapter on Anglican doctrine ought to be the shortest in the book, "for the simple reason that Anglicanism has no doctrines of its own."[142]

English theologian Mark Chapman published, in 2012, a volume titled *Anglican Theology*. In such a book, you might expect to find a systematic, and rigorous, exposition of the subject matter, perhaps beginning with the Anglican doctrine of God, and proceeding to the Anglican doctrine of Christ, and to other Anglican theological particularities, doctrines and beliefs, and so on. But this is not so. Instead, Mark Chapman's book is primarily concerned with history, and more specifically, with how Anglican belief and practice took shape, and was forged, in the context of that history. He addresses these words to his readers at the beginning of his enterprise:

> It is important to point out that those who might be reading this book to find out what Anglicans believe will come away with a good idea of what sorts of things have counted as doing Anglican theology in the past, particularly in the Church of England, and they should come away with a good idea about what some contemporary Anglicans think other Anglicans should believe. But they will be disappointed if they are looking for an Anglican systematic theology. While a few Anglicans

---

142 Giles, *How to be an Anglican*, p. 36.

have written systematic theologies (and it is far fewer than in many other denominations), they have tended to write as theologians who happen to be members of Anglican churches, rather than as Anglican theologians. Anglican theology is thus unlikely to resemble a Lutheran or a Reformed dogmatics. The past functions very differently for most Anglicans: there is no key year or key text. Instead, everything is contested.[143]

The Doctrine Commission of the Church of England addressed this same question in 1938, determining that, "there is not, and the majority of us do not desire that there should be, a system of distinctively Anglican Theology. The Anglican Church receives and holds the faith of Catholic Christendom."[144] What is being said by each of Richard Giles, Mark Chapman, and collectively by the Doctrine Commission of the Church of England in 1938, is that, the Anglican Church, in respect to its doctrine, holds to and affirms the apostolic faith as received and handed down by the early church. The content of this faith has its primary source and authority in Holy Scripture, and is expressed and encapsulated in the ecumenical creeds of the church (The Apostles' and Nicene Creeds), known to, and confessed by, all Christians holding to the same apostolic faith and tradition down through the centuries to the present day.

Whilst the Creeds are, then, the fundamental statements of doctrine known to the Anglican Church, it is also true that during the course of its long history, and especially in the crucible of the sixteenth century Reformation and its aftermath, the Church of England did develop some further, critical statements concerning belief and practice that are in the nature of authoritative theological sources and documents still today. Prominent among these are the 1662 *Book of Common Prayer* inclusive of the Ordinal,

---

143 *Anglican Theology* (London: T&T Clark, 2012), p. 8.
144 Evans & Wright, *A handbook of sources*, p. 401.

and the 39 Articles of Religion, which together constitute distinctively Anglican texts, the content of which has, and continues to the present day, to inform Anglican belief and practice in a variety of important ways.

In the context of the Australian Anglicanism, and its governing documents, these sources of doctrine, belief and practice together shape the form and content of the "Fundamental Declarations" set out in sections 1, 2, and 3 of the constitution of the Anglican Church of Australia. The Fundamental Declarations are, therefore, axiomatic and foundational, and should be carefully read, studied and absorbed in their fullness, by any person considering any form of authorised ministry, lay or ordained, in the Anglican Church of Australia.

The Fundamental Declarations

Succinctly, the Fundamental Declarations require assent to the apostolic faith as summarised by the Apostles' and Nicene Creeds, affirm Holy Scripture as the ultimate rule and standard of faith, and the ongoing importance in the life of the church of the two "gospel sacraments" of Holy Baptism and Holy Communion, together with the existence of the episcopal church structure and three Orders of ministry embodied in the Ordinal.

The Fundamental Declarations read:

1. The Anglican Church of Australia, being a part of the One Holy Catholic and Apostolic Church of Christ, holds the Christian Faith as professed by the Church of Christ from primitive times and in particular as set forth in the creeds known as the Nicene Creed and the Apostles' Creed.

2. This Church receives all the canonical scriptures of the Old and New Testaments as being the ultimate rule and standard of faith

given by inspiration of God and containing all things necessary for salvation.

3. This Church will ever obey the commands of Christ, teach His doctrine, administer His sacraments of Holy Baptism and Holy Communion, follow and uphold His discipline and preserve the three orders of bishops, priests and deacons in the sacred ministry.

These three sections are unchangeable in every respect,[145] except one, being that the name of the church may be changed, and indeed, as we have seen, this occurred in 1981 when the Church of England in Australia formally became the Anglican Church of Australia. The Fundamental Declarations give a clear, and concise, description of the distinctive beliefs and characteristics of the Anglican Church, and point to the sources which inform and shape them.

The "Ruling Principles," set out in sections 4, 5 and 6 of the constitution, further recognise the heritage and legacy of the Australian Church in, and affirm its continuing relationship with, the Church of England in England. Sections 4 and 6 are especially important in this regard.

4. This Church, being derived from the Church of England, retains and approves the doctrine and principles of the Church of England embodied in the Book of Common Prayer with the form and manner of making and ordaining and consecrating Bishops, Priests and Deacons and the Articles of Religion sometimes called the Thirty-Nine Articles.

6. This Church will remain and be in communion with the Church of England and with churches in communion therewith so long

---

145 Constitution of the Anglican Church of Australia s 66.

as communion is consistent with the Fundamental Declarations contained in this Constitution.

These fundamentals reflect the development of the distinctly Anglican form of practice and belief that developed over the course of the long, and often tumultuous, history of the Church of England, and which were transmitted to the Australian context by those who brought the Anglican way to these shores, beginning with Chaplain Johnson who arrived on the first fleet in 1788. As we have seen, any person being ordained in the Anglican Church of Australia is required by canon law to formally declare their assent to, and give a commitment to, these fundamental declarations of faith, in the form prescribed by the *Oaths Affirmations Declarations and Assents Canon 1992*. The Fundamental Declarations can, therefore, be rightly thought of as embodying what they say they are – they are in fact fundamentals, being the absolute and unchangeable foundation upon which the doctrinal and theological edifice of the Anglican Church of Australia rises.

The Ecumenical Creeds

The prominence and importance of the historic Creeds of the church in the Fundamental Declarations, and in other Anglican governing documents and liturgical texts, demonstrate that, whilst many have, and still do, seek to identify and focus on that which is different or distinct about the Anglican Church in relation to other Christian denominations and movements; it is nevertheless true that the most important beliefs for Anglicans are, in fact, shared by, and held in common with, most other Christians. This is because, as Martin Davie explains:

> To understand the origins and the beginnings of the Anglican Church in the midst of all the changes that have taken place in the Church

of England over the course of its history one of the things that has remained constant is its commitment to the faith "uniquely revealed in the Holy Scriptures and set forth in the catholic creeds."[146]

What is being referred to here as "the catholic creeds" are also commonly called "the ecumenical creeds". These are the historic statements of faith developed by the early church at the time when there was only one universal (or "catholic") church, to which all believers, in every part of the world, belonged. Historically, this period of time is that stretching from the beginnings of Christianity itself, broadly until the eventual split, in 1054, between the western church centred on Rome, and the eastern church centred on Constantinople (modern day Istanbul). The historic statements of faith known as the "ecumenical creeds" (because they originated before the division of 1054), are generally agreed to be three in number.

a) The Apostles' Creed. Impossible to date with precision, but a product of the first generations of Christians, purporting to be a summary of the teaching of the original apostles. The Apostles' Creed is used as a symbol of the content of the Christian faith at the services of initiation – baptism and confirmation.

b) The Nicene Creed. Originally adopted by the Council of Nicaea called by the emperor Constantine in 325, and later revised by two further councils in 381 (Constantinople) and 451 (Chalcedon). The Nicene Creed is a continuing and integral part of the liturgy of Holy Communion, usually recited together by the congregation as a summary of the Christian faith ("Let us together affirm the faith of the church…").

---

146 *A guide to the Church of England* (London: Bloomsbury, 2008), p. 80.

c) The Athanasian Creed. The longest of the ecumenical creeds, it is a Trinitarian treatise of uncertain antiquity and origin, that is rarely used today, but can be found in APBA (pp. 487–488).

The ecumenical creeds continue to function as definitive statements and summaries of the Christian faith for Anglicans (as for most other Christians). Hence, the first thing the Anglican Church of Australia says in its constitution is:

> The Anglican Church of Australia, being a part of the One Holy Catholic and Apostolic Church of Christ, holds the Christian Faith as professed by the Church of Christ from primitive times and in particular as set forth in the creeds known as the Nicene Creed and the Apostles' Creed.

It is, in this sense, that it can be said the Anglican Church has no distinctive doctrines of its own, but knows of and adheres only to the faith of the universal (or "catholic") church as set out in the same ecumenical creeds. Because the creeds transcend the Reformation, and were retained as confessional statements by the Church of England, they serve to link the church that emerged from the Reformation with that which had existed before it, and to preserve the historic continuity of the Church of England, and the Anglican churches around the world descended from it, with Jesus and the apostles and with the early church of Christian antiquity. The ecumenical creeds were not the only thing that continued unbroken beyond the Reformation. The third of the fundamental declarations of the Australian church's constitution points to some further points of continuity:

> This Church will ever obey the commands of Christ, teach His doctrine, administer His sacraments of Holy Baptism and Holy

Communion, follow and uphold His discipline and preserve the three orders of bishops, priests and deacons in the sacred ministry.

This statement identifies two continuing distinctive features of the Anglican Church that also transcended the Reformation in a way that was not true of other churches that emerged from that period of history – the ongoing importance of the sacraments (of which there are considered two (Holy Communion and Holy Baptism); and the continued presence of the threefold order of bishops, priests and deacons (the episcopal church structure).

The Primacy of Scripture

Whereas the ecumenical creeds are understood to embody in summary the theological substance of the Christian faith, the Holy Scriptures, meaning the sacred writings contained in the canonical books of the Old and New Testaments, are the ultimate source and authority for matters of faith and practice, and the very foundation upon which everything else, inclusive of the ecumenical creeds, are built. This is clearly affirmed by the Articles of Religion, which understand the ecumenical creeds of the church to have their warrant in, and to therefore derive their authority from, Holy Scripture.

> Article 8. *Of the Creeds*
> The Three Creeds, Nicene Creed, Athanasius' Creed, and that which is commonly called the Apostles' Creed, ought thoroughly to be received and believed: for they may be proved by most certain warrants of Holy Scripture.

The second of the three fundamental declarations of the constitution of the Anglican Church of Australia points to the primacy of Holy Scripture as the "ultimate rule and standard of faith" given by divine inspiration:

> This Church receives all the canonical scriptures of the Old and New Testaments as being the ultimate rule and standard of faith given by inspiration of God and containing all things necessary for salvation.

In this, the constitution echoes the language of the Articles of Religion.

> Article 6. *Of the Sufficiency of the Holy Scriptures for Salvation.*
> Holy Scripture containeth all things necessary to salvation: so that whatsoever is not read therein, nor may be proved thereby, is not to be required of any man, that it should be believed as an article of the Faith, or be thought requisite or necessary to salvation. In the name of the Holy Scripture we do understand those canonical Books of the Old and New Testament, of whose authority was never any doubt in the Church.

Article 6, one of the most well-known and widely referenced of all the Articles, read in conjunction with the fundamental declarations of the constitution, sets out the reasons for, and the manner in which, the Scriptures function as the most important (or "ultimate") source and foundation of belief for Anglicans. The claims made of Holy Scripture in the 39 Articles of Religion, and set out in the fundamental declarations of the constitution of the Anglican Church of Australia, are that:

- The Scriptures are given by and inspired by God. They were not an entirely human work, nor are they like any other form of writing. These are sacred texts, having their source in God, but expressed in and through human agents (writers).

- The Scriptures are defined as the books of the Old and New Testaments (the Bible), whose authority was never in doubt in the church. This is a reference to the early church, which fixed the number and list of the books (called the "canon" meaning "rule" or "standard") around the same time the ecumenical creeds reached their final forms. Article 6 lists which books of the Bible are considered canonical by the Church of England.

- These Scriptures contain "all things necessary to salvation". The result and effect of this famous statement is then spelled out: "so that whatsoever is not read therein, nor may be proved thereby, is not to be required of any man, that it should be believed as an article of the Faith."

The Thirty-Nine Articles of Religion

The 39 Articles of Religion can be found in APBA pp. 476–485. The Articles emerged out of the tumult of the English Reformation, at a time when it became increasingly urgent for the English church, which was emerging out of the separation with the church of Rome, to make some form of a declaration as to where it stood in relation to the many religious and theological controversies of the time.

> In specific terms this meant that it had to define where it stood in relation to the teaching being propagated by those who remained loyal to Rome, by the mainstream Reformers in continental Europe such as Luther, Zwingli, Calvin and Bucer and by the theologians of the radical Reformation both on the continent and at home.[147]

---

147 Martin Davie, *Our inheritance of faith: A commentary on the thirty nine articles* (Gilead Books, 2013), p. 12.

Statements of belief and practice in the form of Articles, in smaller groups of ten (1536), six (1539) and thirteen (1538), were produced by parliaments and the church convocations as the English Reformation developed. The death of Henry VIII, and the accession of the young and frail Edward VI in 1547, provided an opportunity for those English bishops, led by Thomas Cranmer, who wanted to take the English church in an increasingly Protestant direction. This resulted in the publication of the first two Books of Common Prayer in 1549 and 1552, and the first Book of Homilies in 1547. Agreement on a shared statement of faith took longer. Cranmer was working on a document that would ultimately form the basis for his "Forty-Two Articles" from around 1549, for correspondence survives that alludes to this ongoing work.[148] The Forty-Two Articles were eventually published in June 1553, just prior to the death of Edward VI and the accession of his sister Queen Mary, at which time the English church was abruptly, and tumultuously, returned to the authority of the Pope and the Roman church. Upon the death of Queen Mary five years later, and with the accession to the throne of Queen Elizabeth I, attention was returned to the Forty-Two Articles, and a new revision was agreed to in 1563 which reduced the number of Articles to Thirty-Eight, with the final form of the now familiar Thirty-Nine Articles being agreed to and ratified by "the Archbishop and Bishops of the Upper House" and by "the whole Clergy of the Nether House in their Convocation" in 1571.[149]

Although the process of revision was, in some places, extensive, the conception of the Articles, their order, and their "theological personality", which together give them their distinctive character, remained substantially the work of Thomas Cranmer, with the result that Cranmer can be confidently asserted to be, "in effect, the author of our Thirty Nine Articles."[150] The distinctive language and "personality" of the 39 Articles has the effect of distinguishing them among the several great confessions and other doctrinal

---

148 Davie, *Our inheritance of faith*, p. 30.
149 From "The Ratification" as published in the *Book of Common Prayer 1662*.
150 Davie, *Our inheritance of faith*, p. 61.

statements produced over the course of the European Reformation and in its aftermath. A number of different theories and positions have been put forward, over the years, as to the extent to which the 39 Articles reflect a particular theological position, be it Calvinist or Arminian, or other, and the extent to which, or otherwise, they are compatible with a Reformed and a Catholic theology, or with both simultaneously. Perhaps Bruce Kaye summarises the distinctiveness of the Articles best by concluding, they "cannot be described either as Calvinist or Lutheran. They are in fact Anglican."[151]

In totality, the Articles are a collection of affirmations and denials. The denials are, generally, denunciations of aspects of Roman Catholic doctrine (e.g. Article 22, on why purgatory is an inadequate belief), and of some Protestant positions (e.g. Article 27, on the baptism of infants, which some Protestants denied, but which the Articles affirm and the Anglican Church continues to practise). The affirmations within the Articles reside in the many positive statements about the nature of God (Articles 1–5), the reliable sources of faith (Articles 6–8), and on human sin and the remedy for it (Articles 9–12). These are clearly doctrinal statements. A good example is the very first article, which makes some clear and concise statements about the nature and being of God.

> Article I. *Of Faith in the Holy Trinity.*
> There is but one living and true God, everlasting, without body, parts, or passions; of infinite power, wisdom, and goodness; the Maker, and Preserver of all things both visible and invisible. And in unity of this Godhead there be three Persons, of one substance, power, and eternity; the Father, the Son, and the Holy Ghost.

Many of the later Articles are, however, clearly not of a doctrinal nature in substance, but address the social, political, and religious controversies

---

151 *A church without walls*, p. 64.

and disputes of the time. An example of this is Article 38, the purpose of which is to oppose a teaching of some of the more radical Protestant groups (described in the Article as "certain Anabaptists") that Christian people should hold their possessions in common.

> Article 38. *Of Christian Men's Goods, which are not common.*
> The Riches and Goods of Christians are not common, as touching the right, title, and possession of the same; as certain Anabaptists do falsely boast. Notwithstanding, every man ought, of such things as he possesseth, liberally to give alms to the poor, according to his ability.

The Articles (in Article 36) also confirm the retention of the threefold order of bishops, priests and deacons, as promulgated by the Ordinal. This finds expression in the fundamental declarations of the constitution of the Anglican Church of Australia ("this church will ever... preserve the three orders of bishops, priests and deacons in the sacred ministry").

The 39 Articles occupy a place of both historical, and continuing, importance in the Anglican Church. Though they were not intended to constitute a systematic theology, they do cover most of the main areas of Christian belief and practice, and are in this sense confessional and doctrinal. Further, the Articles have a primary application to the ordained clergy of the church, and were intended to set out the limits of acceptable teaching and practice for clergy of the Church of England, and to distinguish between truth and error.[152] All those being ordained in the Anglican Church of Australia (as reflected in the historic and continuing canon law of the Church of England) make a declaration giving their assent to "the doctrine of the Anglican Church of Australia as expressed in the Book of Common Prayer and the Ordering of Bishops, Priests and Deacons ***and the Articles of Religion***, as acknowledged in section 4 of the Constitution."[153]

---

152 Davie, *Our inheritance of faith*, p. 15.
153 The *Oaths Affirmations Declarations and Assents Canon 1992* s 5.

The Book of Common Prayer

The ideal of "common prayer" became a guiding principle in Anglican worship, codified legally by the acts of uniformity passed by the English parliament, which enforced the *Book of Common Prayer* as the sole (and therefore "uniform") text permitted to be used in public acts of worship. There were several such Acts, in 1549, 1552, 1559 and 1662. In each (with the exception of the 1559 Act) the full text of the *Book of Common Prayer* was appended to the legislation. The full title sets out the purpose and effect the *Act of Uniformity* was intended to have:

> An Act For the Uniformity of Publick Prayers; and Administration of Sacraments, and other Rites and Ceremonies: And for establishing the Form of Making, Ordaining, and Consecrating Bishops, Priests, and Deacons in the Church of England. '

Although the 1662 Act only applied to England and Wales, the 1662 *Book of Common Prayer* subsequently acquired an authority in and of itself as the authorised liturgical text of the Anglican church, both in England and Wales, and in most other parts of the world in which Anglican churches were subsequently established.

The very first *Book of Common Prayer* was produced by a group of bishops overseen by Archbishop Thomas Cranmer in 1549, who clearly had a large and influential role in the development of the text and possibly drafted much of it himself.[154] The object of the first *Book of Common Prayer* was to make the public services of worship of the Church of England available in plain, and simple to follow, English language, superseding centuries of the exclusive use of Latin in public worship. The first *Book of Common Prayer* was revised after just three years, with a new Prayer Book, including and

---

154 *Historical dictionary of Anglicanism*, p. 106.

embracing many more of the changes being ushered in by the reformers, being published in 1552. The 1552 Prayer Book was lightly revised in the year after the accession of Queen Elizabeth I (1599), only to then be banned by the Puritans during the course of the English Civil War and made illegal during the Commonwealth period of 1649–1660. Following the restoration of the monarchy in 1660, the *Book of Common Prayer* regained its status as the official and uniform text for Anglican worship via the 1662 *Act of Uniformity* to which its revised form was attached. It is this 1662 *Book of Common Prayer* that is, and remains, *the* Prayer Book for Anglicans both in England and Australia, and in most other parts of the Anglican world.[155]

The 1662 *Book of Common Prayer* is not, despite this somewhat tumultuous history, a substantially new publication, but is the direct descendent of the first two Books of Common Prayer of 1549 and 1552. All are the beneficiaries of the particular genius of Archbishop Thomas Cranmer, whose "desire for radical reform was matched by a gift for beautiful language."[156] That language, together with the shape and form in which it is contained, informs and influences how Anglicans continue to worship to the present day, even if the 1662 book is no longer in common, let alone universal, use. Whilst Cranmer had a large and important role in the production of the *Book of Common Prayer*, to ask who actually wrote the *Book of Common Prayer* is, as Charles Hefling advises, to ask the wrong question.

> For one thing, *compiled* would be a better word than *wrote*. Most of the Prayer Book text is transcribed *verbatim* from the Bible. Some of it is translated from far older liturgical texts. Some of it is on loan, borrowed

---

155 The Constitution of the Anglican Church of Australia s 74(2) makes explicit that a reference to the Book of Common Prayer in the Constitution means the 1662 Prayer Book.

156 Giles, *How to be an Anglican*, p. 65.

and adapted from service books that were being used elsewhere. Some of its formal arrangement is novel, much of it very traditional.[157]

The intent of the various acts of uniformity, and the notion of "common prayer", were to provide for a national church that could hold within its parameters both those who wished to preserve and continue the traditions of the past, and those who wanted to implement the reforms of the recent past more fully. The possibility of walking this middle road and of occupying that middle ground, whilst simultaneously holding together these often-divergent religious traditions and theological positions within the one church, is given its most famous expression in the influential 1597 theological treatise *The Laws of Ecclesiastical Polity* by Richard Hooker (1554–1600). In this seminal work, Hooker builds a foundation of belief and practise, and of church ordering and governance ("polity"), that is constructed around the foundations of scripture, tradition and reason, and which introduces the distinctly Anglican concept of a "middle way" (or *via media*). The conceptual position taken by Hooker was to distinguish the Anglican Church from both the Roman Catholic church and the Puritan Protestants, in a way that maintained the Anglican Church was neither wholly "catholic" nor wholly "reformed", but something else, and which sought to navigate a path that embraces and enjoins much of both, whilst leaving aside the more extreme forms of each.

For many, the "middle way" is a defining feature of Anglicanism. But there has always been, and was always intended to be, limits to the nature of the uniformity and of "common prayer" among the architects of the *Book of Common Prayer*, and more broadly within what might be called the Prayer Book tradition. The Preface to the *Book of Common Prayer*, which was written to set out how it should be understood, attempts to walk a very characteristically Anglican "middle way" between rigidity and flexibility in its opening statement.

---

157 *The Book of Common Prayer: A guide* (Oxford University Press, 2021), p. 90 (emphasis his).

It hath been the wisdom of the Church of England, ever since the first compiling of her Publick Liturgy, to keep the mean between the two extremes, of too much stiffness in refusing, and of too much easiness in admitting any variation from it.

The Articles of Religion further recognise that there are some limits to uniformity, and that not every expression of worship need be the same in every detail.

Article 34. *Of the Traditions of the Church.*
It is not necessary that Traditions and Ceremonies be in all places one, or utterly like; for at all times they have been divers, and may be changed according to the diversity of countries, times, and men's manners, so that nothing be ordained against God's Word... Every particular or national Church hath authority to ordain, change, and abolish, Ceremonies or Rites of the Church ordained only by man's authority, so that all things be done to edifying.

A guiding principle of the Reformation, embraced by the Church of England, and one of the very reasons for which the *Book of Common Prayer* was first produced by Archbishop Cranmer in 1549, was that the language of public worship should be capable of being understood by the greatest number of the people of the day. Clearly, language changes over time, as words lose their meaning or acquire new meanings. As beautifully poetic and majestic as it is, no one, in everyday life today, writes or speaks English in the same way it was written and spoken at the time the *Book of Common Prayer* was produced. As an ideal and a principle, common prayer was not intended to be a relic of the past, but a living thing, capable of adapting to the host culture and of both enriching it and of being enriched by it.

The importance of the principle of common prayer in the Anglican Church, therefore, goes beyond preserving the form of words in the liturgy, but points to one of the defining and distinguishing features of Anglicanism itself. Indeed, some have even suggested that, in essence, Anglicanism is, in fact, essentially "a way of worship".

> The Book of Common Prayer is far more than the words between the covers of the book. Its texts and directions for ordering worship point to a living tradition, to a distinct way of being Christian. The Prayer Book has been revised repeatedly over the course of its history... but in every revision there are principles, values, and theological perspectives that mark the identity of Anglican corporate prayer... If you ask an Anglican what it means to belong to the church, the answer might well be, "Come and worship with us."[158]

The *Book of Common Prayer* can be, and often is, described as a doctrinal text. This is not so much because the Prayer Book contains doctrinal statements about what Christians believe, such as the creeds and a catechism, although it certainly does; but because it is in the context of public worship, and in and through the words used, and the forms of the rites and ceremonies prescribed by the Prayer Book, that Anglicans, both individually and together, profess their faith. This has often been summed up, as we saw, in the Latin catchcry *lex orandi, lex credenda* ("what we pray, we believe"). As Samuel Wells concludes in his study of what Anglicans believe, "if there were one symbol of the convergence of Scripture, tradition and reason, it would be the Book of Common Prayer."[159]

Although there is much more that could be said and written about the nature and conduct of Anglican worship, and indeed many books and essays have been composed on the subject over the years, there are some principles bequeathed by the notion of "common prayer" that normally

---

158 Jeffrey Lee, *Opening the Prayer Book* (Cambridge, MA: Cowley, 1999), p. 7.
159 *What Anglicans believe: an introduction* (Norwich: The Canterbury Press, 2011), p. 68.

mean Anglican services of worship anywhere in the world will bear some form of "family likeness" to each other. This is the very nature of "common prayer". Whilst this is also often very keenly contested ground, some of the elements common to Anglican worship might include one or more of those articulated below by liturgical theologian Colin Buchanan.[160]

- The rhythms of the church year are present, at least in regard to the major festivals.

- A pattern of reading scripture systematically, often with reference to the lectionary, is followed.

- Certain set forms of prayer that are said together by all, such as the Lord's Prayer and some other prayers often called "collects" will be part of the service.

- The sacraments of Holy Baptism and Holy Communion are accepted as having biblical warrant, and practised.

- The worship is in a form able to be readily understood, and which enables participation.

The nature of Anglican worship, with set forms of prayers and other participatory aspects, and directive rubrics regarding posture and other elements of the service, is often described as "liturgical", in that much of what is said and done, is said and done "by the book". This, coupled with the historic tendency for the English church to be well ordered and dignified, has led many Anglicans to claim a high degree of concurrence with the

---

[160] In Adrian Chatfield (Ed. David Payne), *Something in common: an introduction to the principles and practises of worldwide Anglicanism* (Bramcote, Nottingham: St John's College, 1998), p. 33.

direction of Paul, regarding the conduct of the gatherings of believers in ancient Corinth, that "all things should be done decently and in order" (1 Corinthians 14.40).

Finally, it is important to note and understand that the 1662 *Book of Common Prayer* remains the authoritative source for liturgy in the Anglican Church of Australia, and that this is embedded in the constitution of the Anglican Church of Australia. This is because the reference to the *Book of Common Prayer* in the ruling principles of the constitution of the Anglican Church of Australia (s 4), that, "this Church, being derived from the Church of England, retains and approves the doctrine and principles of the Church of England embodied in the Book of Common Prayer", means the 1662 *Book of Common Prayer*. Whilst there are many Prayer Books in use around the Anglican world, and now three liturgical books authorised by the church for use in public worship in the Anglican Church of Australia (the *Book of Common Prayer 1662*, *An Australian Prayer Book 1978*, and *A Prayer Book for Australia 1995*), the 1662 *Book of Common Prayer*, consistent with the fundamental declarations of the constitution of the Anglican Church of Australia, remains the foundation and the benchmark.

The instruments of communion

By the late nineteenth century, churches descended from the Church of England had been established, and were flourishing, in many parts of the world, especially in those parts of the world directly affected by the expansion of the British Empire across the globe, and by the missionary activity that frequently followed it. The question of what relationship the churches descended from the Church of England in different parts of the world bore to the "mother church" in England, and in what sense each were recognisably Anglican and could be identified as such, became increasingly important.

The essential elements of the shared belief and practice, and ethos, held in common by the various expression of Anglicanism around the world was eventually distilled into the form of the so-called Chicago-Lambeth Quadrilateral. The Quadrilateral has its origins at a meeting of Anglican bishops from around the world held in Chicago in 1886, and takes its name from the four statements proposed by the meeting as constituting the essential and defining features of Anglicanism. These were adopted, with some very minor modification, at a further meeting of the bishops from around the Anglican Communion at the Lambeth conference (so-called as it was initially held at Lambeth Palace, the London residence of the Archbishop of Canterbury) in 1888.

The Chicago-Lambeth Quadrilateral, as adopted at Lambeth in 1888, states the basis of unity as:

a) The Holy Scriptures of the Old and New Testaments, as "containing all things necessary to salvation," and as being the rule and ultimate standard of faith.

b) The Apostles' Creed, as the Baptismal Symbol; and the Nicene Creed, as the sufficient statement of the Christian faith.

c) The two Sacraments ordained by Christ Himself – Baptism and the Supper of the Lord – ministered with unfailing use of Christ's words of Institution, and of the elements ordained by Him.

d) The Historic Episcopate, locally adapted in the methods of its administration to the varying needs of the nations and peoples called of God into the Unity of His Church.

The Chicago-Lambeth Quadrilateral sets out, in a very minimalist way, the foundations of belief and practise that are common to Anglican churches around the world. Collectively, this family of churches, and the people who comprise them, is known as the (global) Anglican Communion. The 1930 Lambeth Conference defined the Anglican Communion as:

> A fellowship within the one holy catholic and apostolic church, of those duly constituted dioceses, provinces or regional churches in communion with the see of Canterbury.

Today, the Anglican Communion consists of many millions of adherents and is present in the vast majority of the nations of the world. The Anglican Communion has identified four "Instruments of Communion" that define it internationally. These are:

1) The office of the Archbishop of Canterbury;

2) The Lambeth Conference, which usually takes place every ten years, with bishops from around the Anglican world attending;

3) The Primates' Meeting, comprising the chief Archbishops, Presiding Bishops, Moderators and chief pastors of the more than 40 Anglican provinces around the world;

4) The Anglican Consultative Council, comprised of clerical and lay members from around the Communion, and which serves the needs of member churches.

Postscript – the testing of vocation

In his important and broad study of the laws of Christian churches of all traditions from around the world, Norman Doe finds that "all churches agree that there is no right to ordination."[161] This stark reality is a starting point for every vocational conversation. There is no inherent right to ordination, and no one is entitled to demand it, no matter how clearly and how strongly a particular person may profess to hear such a call, nor how vigorously it is contended for. The most anyone can ever do is to express a sense of call, and request that their sense of vocation arising out of that conviction be tested by the formal processes in place in that church context. The former can be done assertively, and often is, but the latter always puts the person professing a call, however assertively, into a vulnerable position.

The process applied by a particular diocese and its leader, the diocesan bishop, for discerning a vocation to ordained ministry may vary from national church to national church across the Anglican communion, and from diocese to diocese across the Anglican Church of Australia. That process will usually, at an early stage, take into consideration the advice of the candidate's minister, often their vicar or a chaplain, who knows them well and has observed them at local level. A person at diocesan level, whether a vocational adviser or another such person or the bishop themself, will then meet the candidate to discuss their aspiration and calling. There may, then, be a formal discernment program the candidate is invited to join.

This may then lead to the involvement of others given the task of

---

161 *Christian law*, p. 78.

conducting formal interviews on behalf of the wider church, often called examining chaplains. There will be a safeguarding or clearance process, entailing background checks, referees, and possibly more, that will be thorough in most instances, and will take some time to complete. In many places the candidate will be asked to make a formal application using a prescribed form. A general medical examination may be requested, and there may be one or more psychological evaluations conducted by a qualified person. Finally, it is likely there will be a formal selection process that will involve the convening of a panel of interviewers, charged with the task of testing the candidate's vocation on behalf of the wider church, and of making a recommendation to the decision maker, who will be the diocesan bishop or Archbishop of that diocese. This reflects the widely recognised and practised "general principle of Anglican canon law that the right to determine suitability of candidates for ordination as priests and deacons rests with the bishop."[162]

The whole process, that may last over the course of several months, and sometimes longer, should be thought of in terms of a journey, rather than an examination, although it may feel like the latter. The journey is one of discernment, undertaken with others. Many on this journey of discernment may decide not to proceed to the point of decision, and may not, then, submit themselves to a formal selection process. Or they may decide the time is not right, and instead resolve to wait on the Lord a little longer. Others may choose to proceed and to formally test their vocation by submitting themselves to the corporate wisdom of the church as determined by the selection process. In most selection processes, there are three possible recommendations that might be made to the diocesan bishop in relation to an individual candidate's vocation to ordained ministry – a vocation to ordained ministry is affirmed, a vocation to ordained ministry is not affirmed and the candidate is affirmed in their

---

162 Doe & Ombres, 'The ministry of clergy in Anglican and Roman Catholic canon law,' p. 7.

lay ministry, or there may be a "not yet" coupled with an invitation to return for consideration at a later time.

When the church says "no"

The church never says "no" to ministry, because all the baptised have a ministry in God's church and are engaged in the ministry of reconciliation and furtherance of God's kingdom on earth. One possible outcome of a selection process, however, is that a candidate is not recommended for the ordained ministry, but is instead affirmed in their lay ministry and encouraged to continue to be engaged in Christian ministry in a lay capacity. Another way of putting this is that the outcome at selection is that a vocation to ordained ministry could not be affirmed by the selectors. The reality is that this is often received as a "no", and frequently a very painful "no", as the person expressing a vocation to ordained ministry is doing so out of a personal sense of calling, often very strongly felt and experienced, that the representatives of the church have not been able to reciprocate. As painful as this is to hear, receive and process, a further reality is that any person submitting themselves to a selection process must be prepared to receive this answer.

The sense of rejection a candidate who has put themselves forward in good faith and out of a genuine sense of vocation may feel when receiving a "no" is often compounded by the inability of the selectors, or of their representative, whether the diocesan bishop or a diocesan officer such as a vocations adviser or similar, to provide reasons, or to be in a position only to provide superficial ones. This is because there are pastoral implications, sometimes severe, in betraying a confidence arising out of a reference, for example, and frequently also considerations around confidentiality for people involved in the process. Sometimes there may be professional standards matters pertaining to the candidate's ability to obtain the necessary clearances that cannot be divulged. Most of the time, however, at least in my experience, the reality is that what we describe as a sense of calling by God and of a resulting experience of a vocation to ordained ministry is an inherently spiritual and intangible thing. It can be difficult to put into words why the church's representative persons cannot see and experience what the candidate can see and experience. This can be frustrating and difficult for all concerned.

> In most contexts there is no intention of inflicting pain, but individuals who have not been chosen often feel themselves misrepresented, misunderstood or unvalued by "them". They experience real pain. The powerlessness to redress outcomes or have questions answered compounds the felling of the selecting body as victimizers.[163]

It is important to appreciate that, in most selection processes and certainly the ones I am familiar with, the "no" is never usually the decision of a single person, but a corporate "no" shared by a number of selectors, interviewers, referees, various professional persons, and others involved along the way. It can be thought of as a corporate and cumulative outcome. The other side of this is that the reception of the "no" is never usually an individual event either. The pain of the rejection felt by such an outcome is often shared by others, and sometimes many others, including family members, mentors, friends and colleagues, and sometimes an entire parish community or congregation who have together sponsored the candidate in their journey towards selection.

Most selectors, both individually and corporately, will acknowledge the fallibility of human discernment in light of the perfection of God. It is true in the Scriptures that, in the divine prerogative, God both chooses and rejects.[164] The divine prerogative is perfect, but the human discernment

---

163 Helen Thorp, *When the church says no* (Grove Books, 2004), p. 5.
164 Genesis 4.1-5; 1 Samuel 15.26-28; 1 Samuel 16.1-7; Acts 1.23-26, 13.2, 15.22.

of that divine prerogative is not. The possibility that the church has got it wrong always exists. The most compelling example is that of Christ himself, who submitted himself always to the divine will, even in the light of human rejection and the experience of the abandonment of God on the cross (Mark 15.34). For the person of Jesus, both self-worth and approval came from God, and have their location in the divine rather than the human. He found his sense of comfort and peace in knowing who he was, as a child of the living God. It is in this indelible sense of belonging to God, and of both knowing God and being known by God, that we find our worth, our belonging, and our very being. No decision by a human or panel of humans, however difficult to hear and experience, can change that spiritual truth.

In an article for the *Church Times* in 2017 the leading vocations adviser for the Church of England's national Ministry Division, Catherine Nancekievell, recalled and reflected on feeling "heartbroken" after being "turned down" for ordination. She writes, "after many months, the grey fog of hurt started to lift. I found that, instead of the previous sense of heading towards something, there was just me and God. Not me and God and ordination. I felt freer, more confident in my faith."[165] Whilst acknowledging that it was painful and difficult to hear the answer "no", Nancekievell concludes that the selectors "did get it right."[166]

When the church says "not yet"

A conditional answer, which is often ambiguous or received as such, can be more difficult than a "no". A "no" is usually definitive, at least for the foreseeable future. A "not yet" or an outcome that is expressed in terms of doubt or uncertainty in respect to a professed vocation to ordained

---

165 "A vocation, but not that one," *Church Times* 07 July 2017.
166 "A vocation, but not that one," *Church Times* 07 July 2017.

ministry, may or may not have attached to it the possibility of returning to consideration at a future time.

There are multiple reasons for this outcome, which in my experience of the selection process, is usually avoided unless those tasked with discernment find themselves unable to give any other response. It may be that the selectors were divided and unable to reach consensus. It may be that there is something further needed from the candidate. Often the critical need is time. This is especially true of those who may be recent joiners in respect to the Anglican tradition. A common dilemma for selectors in this post-denominational age is what answer to give often wonderfully gifted and experienced men and women who are coming before selection panels expressing a vocation to a tradition in which they are not yet fully formed, generally through the brevity of time they have been involved in an Anglican context. Put another way, the question selectors often wrestle with is to what extent a person who has had limited experience and opportunity in the Anglican tradition can discern and express a lifelong vocation to ordained ministry in that same tradition. There really is no substitute for sustained participation in the liturgies of the church, and the exercising of the discipline of daily morning and evening prayer, over an extended period of time, to really inhabit the Anglican tradition.

For the candidate receiving an uncertain answer, the primary emotional response can be one of confusion and uncertainty. This is especially exacerbated where there may be a lack of clarity about when to return to selection, or about what else needs to be done or in evidence before returning, or how much time may need to pass before revisiting the vocational question. The fruit of the spirit most needed in such situations is patience (Galatians 5.22), and the most pressing need is one of sustained, diligent prayer for that virtue.

One candidate[167] came forward to selection with great enthusiasm,

---

167 The details recited here are not specific to, or true of, any one person, but reflect in part the stories of several different persons, conflated here for reasons of confidentiality.

and with a conviction that exuded surety and confidence in the outcome. This person was relatively young in years, but had achieved much in both academia and in the context of an early professional career. If selected, and ultimately ordained, this candidate would no doubt go on to serve the church in ministry for decades, probably in senior leadership positions. What looked on paper an easy decision became, around the selection table, a vexed and difficult one. There was something intangible, and difficult to put into words, holding back some, but not all, of those charged with the burden of discernment from speaking a "yes". It was not the candidate's age, but essentially an intuition or spiritual insight. Eventually the answer was "no" but with an invitation to return to selection at a later time if the candidate continued to experience a call to ordained ministry in the future. The candidate received that news with shock and bewilderment. It would be nearly five years before the person concerned returned to a selection process. A little older, much wiser, and in every respect more mature, and more ready. In hindsight, with the benefit of those years, that candidate reflected on the experience of being told "not yet". The intervening years had proved that the decision was the right one, both for the candidate and for the church. In the candidate's own words, "it would have been a disaster" to have proceeded to ordination too quickly. The spiritual insight of the selectors was accurate. But it was only with the benefit of hindsight, and of time, and a good deal of patience on the part of the candidate concerned, that this could be seen with clarity.

When the church says "yes"

In circumstances where the outcome of a selection process is able to add the "yes" of the church to the "yes" of the candidate in respect to the question of a vocation to ordained ministry, that "yes" will never be unconditional. As the Scriptures themselves advise us, "do not ordain anyone hastily" (1 Timothy 5.22), or as another version puts it, "do not be too hasty in the laying on of hands". The "yes" of the church will often be followed by a sentence to the effect of, "and I or we ask you to now do this... or that..." and so on. The "this" and "that" may be a course of academic study or some further units of academic study; it may be to put in place a ministry placement; arrange for a supervisor, mentor or ministry coach; or it may be to undertake a unit of Clinical Pastoral Education (CPE). There will certainly be a safeguarding process to pass through, which will require background checks, reference checks, and providing evidence of safe ministry training, working with children checks, and police checks, if these have not already been done. Even if they have been done, they may well need to be repeated closer to the scheduled date of the ordination. As ordination is intended to be indelible and lifelong, the due diligence conducted by the church and its officers will, rightly, be thorough, and the standards to reach will be high. There will be different things to do and to experience, and to gain proficiency in, prior to ordination proceeding, depending on the context and the diocese in which ordination is to take place, and depending on the individual candidate and their own life, ministry and educational experience. How long the period of time will be, between the selectors' corporate "yes" and the actual ordination, depends on all these variables.

Finally, as indicated previously, there is no guarantee of, nor any right to, ordination. In some places there will be a process applied to assess readiness to proceed to ordination as the date approaches. A possible answer is that there is not sufficient evidence of preparedness, or that something is not yet in place, or still to be undertaken, that ought to be, prior to ordination proceeding. Every candidate will need to take the oath, and make the declarations, required by canon law. As set out in a prior section, every candidate must also have a ministry context to be licensed to, and in which to serve, after ordination. Even if everything falls into place, it is still possible that ordination may be delayed during the course of the actual service itself, for the ordaining bishop is required by the Ordinal to ask the congregation, before the laying on of hands proceeds:

> Dear friends in Christ, you know the importance of this office. We have been assured that these persons are suited to this ministry. If, however, any of you know an adequate reason why we should not proceed, come forward and make it known.[168]

Not alone

Finally, in the church, there is usually always a communal context into which decisions are received and processed. A "yes", "not yet", or "no", will never be heard in isolation.

For most persons of Christian faith, there will be a gathered community, a congregation or worshipping community, there will be leaders ordained and lay, mentors, spiritual advisers and directors, family and friends, many and possibly all of whom will share with the candidate in the joy, frustration or pain of the outcome at selection, and who will be present to offer comfort, prayer, fellowship and support for whatever the path that lies ahead may be.

And, of course, God is always with us, in moments of triumph, confusion and despair, and through whatever life may have store for us. For if we know just one thing as persons of Christian faith, it is that the promise of the one who has said, "I will never leave you or forsake you" (Hebrews 13.5) can be relied on as entirely sure and certain.

---

168 APBA, p. 784.

APPENDICES

Appendix 1
The Fundamental Declarations and Ruling Principles, from the Constitution of the Anglican Church of Australia

Chapter 1 – Fundamental declarations

1. The Anglican Church of Australia, being a part of the One Holy Catholic and Apostolic Church of Christ, holds the Christian Faith as professed by the Church of Christ from primitive times and in particular as set forth in the creeds known as the Nicene Creed and the Apostles' Creed.

2. This Church receives all the canonical scriptures of the Old and New Testaments as being the ultimate rule and standard of faith given by inspiration of God and containing all things necessary for salvation.

3. This Church will ever obey the commands of Christ, teach His doctrine, administer His sacraments of Holy Baptism and Holy Communion, follow and uphold His discipline and preserve the three orders of bishops, priests and deacons in the sacred ministry.

Chapter 2 – Ruling principles [extract]

4. This Church, being derived from the Church of England, retains and approves the doctrine and principles of the Church of England embodied in the Book of Common Prayer together with the Form and Manner of Making Ordaining and Consecrating of Bishops, Priests and Deacons and in the Articles of Religion sometimes called the Thirty-nine Articles but has plenary authority at its own discretion to make statements as to the faith ritual ceremonial or discipline of this Church and to order its forms of worship and rules of discipline and to alter or revise such statements, forms and rules, provided that all such statements, forms, rules or alteration or revision thereof are consistent with the Fundamental Declarations contained herein and are made as prescribed by this Constitution. Provided, and it is hereby further declared, that the above-named Book of Common Prayer, together with the Thirty-nine Articles, be regarded as the authorised standard of worship and doctrine in this Church, and no alteration in or permitted variations from the services or Articles therein contained shall contravene any principle of doctrine or worship laid down in such standard.

5. Subject to the Fundamental Declarations and the provisions of this chapter this Church has plenary authority and power to make canons, ordinances and rules for the order and good government of the Church, and to administer the affairs thereof. Such authority and power may be exercised by the several synods and tribunals in accordance with the provisions of this Constitution.

6. This Church will remain and be in communion with the Church of England in England and with churches in communion therewith so long as communion is consistent with the Fundamental Declarations contained in this Constitution.

Appendix 2
The Apostles' Creed

I believe in God, the Father almighty,
creator of heaven and earth.
I believe in Jesus Christ, God's only Son, our Lord,
who was conceived by the Holy Spirit,
born of the virgin Mary,
suffered under Pontius Pilate,
was crucified, died, and was buried;
he descended to the dead.
On the third day he rose from the dead;
he ascended into heaven,
and is seated at the right hand of the Father;
from there he will come to judge
the living and the dead.
I believe in the Holy Spirit,
the holy catholic Church,
the communion of saints,
the forgiveness of sins,
the resurrection of the body,
and the life everlasting. Amen.
A Prayer Book for Australia 1995.

Appendix 3
The Nicene Creed

We believe in one God,
the Father, the almighty,
maker of heaven and earth,
of all that is, seen and unseen.
We believe in one Lord, Jesus Christ,
the only Son of God,
eternally begotten of the Father,
God from God, Light from Light,
true God from true God,
begotten, not made,
of one being with the Father;
through him all things were made.
For us and for our salvation
he came down from heaven,
was incarnate of the Holy Spirit and the virgin Mary
and became truly human.
For our sake he was crucified under Pontius Pilate;
he suffered death and was buried.
On the third day he rose again
in accordance with the Scriptures;
he ascended into heaven
and is seated at the right hand of the Father.
He will come again in glory to judge

the living and the dead
and his kingdom will have no end.
We believe in the Holy Spirit, the Lord, the giver of life,
who proceeds from the Father and the Son,
who with the Father and the Son
is worshipped and glorified,
who has spoken through the prophets.
We believe in one holy catholic and apostolic Church.
We acknowledge one baptism for the
forgiveness of sins.
We look for the resurrection of the dead,
and the life of the world to come. Amen.
A Prayer Book for Australia 1995.

Appendix 4
The Thirty-Nine Articles of Religion

I. *Of Faith in the Holy Trinity.*
There is but one living and true God, everlasting, without body, parts, or passions; of infinite power, wisdom, and goodness; the Maker, and Preserver of all things both visible and invisible. And in unity of this Godhead there be three Persons, of one substance, power, and eternity; the Father, the Son, and the Holy Ghost.

II. *Of the Word or Son of God, which was made very Man.*
The Son, which is the Word of the Father, begotten from everlasting of the Father, the very and eternal God, and of one substance with the Father, took Man's nature in the womb of the blessed Virgin, of her substance: so that two whole and perfect Natures, that is to say, the Godhead and Manhood, were joined together in one Person, never to be divided, whereof is one Christ, very God, and very Man; who truly suffered, was crucified, dead and buried, to reconcile his Father to us, and to be a sacrifice, not only for original guilt, but also for all actual sins of men.

III. *Of the going down of Christ into Hell.*
As Christ died for us, and was buried, so also is it to be believed, that he went down into Hell.

IV. *Of the Resurrection of Christ.*
Christ did truly rise again from death, and took again his body, with flesh,

bones, and all things appertaining to the perfection of Man's nature; wherewith he ascended into Heaven, and there sitteth, until he return to judge all Men at the last day.

V. *Of the Holy Ghost.*
The Holy Ghost, proceeding from the Father and the Son, is of one substance, majesty, and glory, with the Father and the Son, very and eternal God.

VI. *Of the Sufficiency of the Holy Scriptures for salvation.*
Holy Scripture containeth all things necessary to salvation: so that whatsoever is not read therein, nor may be proved thereby, is not to be required of any man, that it should be believed as an article of the Faith, or be thought requisite or necessary to salvation. In the name of the Holy Scripture we do understand those Canonical Books of the Old and New Testament, of whose authority was never any doubt in the Church. Of the Names and Number of the Canonical Books.

>   Genesis,
>   Exodus,
>   Leviticus,
>   Numbers,
>   Deuteronomy,
>   Joshua,
>   Judges,
>   Ruth,
>   The First Book of Samuel,
>   The Second Book of Samuel,
>   The First Book of Kings,
>   The Second Book of Kings,
>   The First Book of Chronicles,

The Second Book of Chronicles,
The First Book of Esdras,
The Second Book of Esdras,
The Book of Esther,
The Book of Job,
The Psalms,
The Proverbs,
Ecclesiastes or Preacher,
Cantica, or Songs of Solomon,
Four Prophets the greater,
Twelve Prophets the less.

And the other Books (as Hierome saith) the Church doth read for example of life and instruction of manners; but yet doth it not apply them to establish any doctrine; such are these following:

The Third Book of Esdras,
The Fourth Book of Esdras,
The Book of Tobias,
The Book of Judith,
The rest of the Book of Esther,
The Book of Wisdom,
Jesus the Son of Sirach,
Baruch the Prophet,
The Song of the Three Children,
The Story of Susannah,
Of Bel and the Dragon,
The Prayer of Manasses,
The First Book of Maccabees,
The Second Book of Maccabees.

All the Books of the New Testament, as they are commonly received, we do receive, and account them Canonical.

VII. *Of the Old Testament.*
The Old Testament is not contrary to the New: for both in the Old and New Testament everlasting life is offered to Mankind by Christ, who is the only Mediator between God and Man, being both God and Man. Wherefore they are not to be heard, which feign that the old Fathers did look only for transitory promises. Although the Law given from God by Moses, as touching Ceremonies and Rites, do not bind Christian men, nor the Civil precepts thereof ought of necessity to be received in any commonwealth; yet notwithstanding, no Christian man whatsoever is free from the obedience of the Commandments which are called Moral.

VIII. *Of the Three Creeds.*
The Three Creeds, Nicene Creed, Athanasius's Creed, and that which is commonly called the Apostles' Creed, ought thoroughly to be received and believed: for they may be proved by most certain warrants of Holy Scripture.

IX. *Of Original or Birth-sin.*
Original Sin standeth not in the following of Adam, (as the Pelagians do vainly talk;) but it is the fault and corruption of the Nature of every man, that naturally is ingendered of the offspring of Adam; whereby man is very far gone from original righteousness, and is of his own nature inclined to evil, so that the flesh lusteth always contrary to the spirit; and therefore in every person born into this world, it deserveth God's wrath and damnation. And this infection of nature doth remain, yea in them that are regenerated; whereby the lust of the flesh, called in the Greek, *phronema sarkos*, which some do expound the wisdom, some sensuality, some the affection, some the desire, of the flesh, is not subject to the Law of God. And although there is no condemnation for them that believe

and are baptized, yet the Apostle doth confess, that concupiscence and lust hath of itself the nature of sin.

X. *Of Free-Will.*
The condition of Man after the fall of Adam is such, that he cannot turn and prepare himself, by his own natural strength and good works, to faith, and calling upon God: Wherefore we have no power to do good works pleasant and acceptable to God, without the grace of God by Christ preventing us, that we may have a good will, and working with us, when we have that good will.

XI. *Of the Justification of Man.*
We are accounted righteous before God, only for the merit of our Lord and Saviour Jesus Christ by Faith, and not for our own works or deservings: Wherefore, that we are justified by Faith only is a most wholesome Doctrine, and very full of comfort, as more largely is expressed in the Homily of Justification.

XII. *Of Good Works.*
Albeit that Good Works, which are the fruits of Faith, and follow after Justification, cannot put away our sins, and endure the severity of God's Judgement; yet are they pleasing and acceptable to God in Christ, and do spring out necessarily of a true and lively Faith; insomuch that by them a lively Faith may be as evidently known as a tree discerned by the fruit.

XIII. *Of Works before Justification.*
Works done before the grace of Christ, and the Inspiration of his Spirit, are not pleasant to God, forasmuch as they spring not of faith in Jesus Christ, neither do they make men meet to receive grace, or (as the School-authors say) deserve grace of congruity: yea rather, for that they are not done as God hath willed and commanded them to be done, we doubt not but they have the nature of sin.

XIV. *Of Works of Supererogation.*

Voluntary Works besides, over and above, God's Commandments, which they call Works of Supererogation, cannot be taught without arrogancy and impiety: for by them men do declare, that they do not only render unto God as much as they are bound to do, but that they do more for his sake, than of bounden duty is required: whereas Christ saith plainly, When ye have done all that are commanded to you, say, We are unprofitable servants.

XV. *Of Christ alone without Sin.*

Christ in the truth of our nature was made like unto us in all things, sin only except, from which he was clearly void, both in his flesh, and in his spirit. He came to be the Lamb without spot, who, by sacrifice of himself once made, should take away the sins of the world, and sin, as Saint John saith, was not in him. But all we the rest, although baptized, and born again in Christ, yet offend in many things; and if we say we have no sin, we deceive ourselves, and the truth is not in us.

XVI. *Of Sin after Baptism.*

Not every deadly sin willingly committed after Baptism is sin against the Holy Ghost, and unpardonable. Wherefore the grant of repentance is not to be denied to such as fall into sin after Baptism. After we have received the Holy Ghost, we may depart from grace given, and fall into sin, and by the grace of God we may arise again, and amend our lives. And therefore they are to be condemned, which say, they can no more sin as long as they live here, or deny the place of forgiveness to such as truly repent.

XVII. *Of Predestination and Election.*

Predestination to Life is the everlasting purpose of God, whereby (before the foundations of the world were laid) he hath constantly decreed by his counsel secret to us, to deliver from curse and damnation those whom he hath chosen in Christ out of mankind, and to bring them by Christ to everlasting salvation, as vessels made to honour. Wherefore, they which be endued with so excellent a benefit of God be called according to God's purpose by his Spirit working in due season: they through Grace obey the calling: they be justified freely: they be made sons of God by adoption: they be made like the image of his only-begotten Son Jesus Christ: they walk religiously in good works, and at length, by God's mercy, they attain to everlasting felicity.

As the godly consideration of Predestination, and our Election in Christ, is full of sweet, pleasant, and unspeakable comfort to godly persons, and such as feel in themselves the working of the Spirit of Christ, mortifying the works of the flesh, and their earthly members, and drawing up their mind to high and heavenly things, as well because it doth greatly establish and confirm their faith of eternal Salvation to be enjoyed through Christ, as because it doth fervently kindle their love towards God: So, for curious and carnal persons, lacking the Spirit of Christ, to have continually before their eyes the sentence of God's Predestination, is a most dangerous downfall, whereby the Devil doth thrust them either into desperation, or into wretchlessness of most unclean living, no less perilous than desperation.

Furthermore, we must receive God's promises in such wise, as they be generally set forth to us in Holy Scripture: and, in our doings, that Will of God is to be followed, which we have expressly declared unto us in the Word of God.

XVIII. *Of obtaining eternal Salvation only by the Name of Christ.*
They also are to be had accursed that presume to say, That every man shall be saved by the Law or Sect which he professeth, so that he be diligent to frame his life according to that Law, and the light of Nature. For Holy Scripture doth set out unto us only the Name of Jesus Christ, whereby men must be saved.

XIX. *Of the Church.*

The visible Church of Christ is a congregation of faithful men, in the which the pure Word of God is preached, and the Sacraments be duly ministered according to Christ's ordinance in all those things that of necessity are requisite to the same.

As the Church of Jerusalem, Alexandria, and Antioch, have erred; so also the Church of Rome hath erred, not only in their living and manner of Ceremonies, but also in matters of Faith.

XX. *Of the Authority of the Church.*

The Church hath power to decree Rites or Ceremonies, and authority in Controversies of Faith: And yet it is not lawful for the Church to ordain any thing that is contrary to God's Word written, neither may it so expound one place of Scripture, that it be repugnant to another. Wherefore, although the Church be a witness and a keeper of Holy Writ, yet, as it ought not to decree any thing against the same, so besides the same ought it not to enforce any thing to be believed for necessity of Salvation.

XXI. *Of the Authority of General Councils.*

General Councils may not be gathered together without the commandment and will of Princes. And when they be gathered together, (forasmuch as they be an assembly of men, whereof all be not governed with the Spirit and Word of God,) they may err, and sometimes have erred, even in things pertaining unto God. Wherefore things ordained by them as necessary to salvation have neither strength nor authority, unless it may be declared that they be taken out of Holy Scripture.

XXII. *Of Purgatory.*

The Romish Doctrine concerning Purgatory, Pardons, Worshipping and Adoration, as well of Images as of Reliques, and also invocation of Saints, is a fond thing vainly invented, and grounded upon no warranty of Scripture, but rather repugnant to the Word of God.

XXIII. *Of Ministering in the Congregation.*
It is not lawful for any man to take upon him the office of publick preaching, or ministering the Sacraments in the Congregation, before he be lawfully called, and sent to execute the same. And those we ought to judge lawfully called and sent, which be chosen and called to this work by men who have publick authority given unto them in the Congregation, to call and send Ministers into the Lord's vineyard.

XXIV. *Of speaking in the Congregation in such a tongue as the people understandeth.*
It is a thing plainly repugnant to the Word of God, and the custom of the Primitive Church, to have publick Prayer in the Church, or to minister the Sacraments in a tongue not understanded of the people.

XXV. *Of the Sacraments.*
Sacraments ordained of Christ be not only badges or tokens of Christian men's profession, but rather they be certain sure witnesses, and effectual signs of grace, and God's good will towards us, by the which he doth work invisibly in us, and doth not only quicken, but also strengthen and confirm our Faith in him.

There are two Sacraments ordained of Christ our Lord in the Gospel, that is to say, Baptism, and the Supper of the Lord.

Those five commonly called Sacraments, that is to say, Confirmation, Penance, Orders, Matrimony, and extreme Unction, are not to be counted for Sacraments of the Gospel, being such as have grown partly of the corrupt following of the Apostles, partly are states of life allowed in the Scriptures; but yet have not like nature of Sacraments with Baptism, and the Lord's Supper, for that they have not any visible sign or ceremony ordained of God.

The Sacraments were not ordained of Christ to be gazed upon, or to be carried about, but that we should duly use them. And in such only as worthily receive the same they have a wholesome effect or operation: but they that receive them unworthily purchase to themselves damnation, as Saint Paul saith.

XXVI. *Of the Unworthiness of the Ministers, which hinders not the effect of the Sacrament.*
Although in the visible Church the evil be ever mingled with the good, and sometimes the evil have chief authority in the Ministration of the Word and Sacraments, yet forasmuch as they do not the same in their own name, but in Christ's, and do minister by his commission and authority, we may use their Ministry, both in hearing the Word of God, and in receiving of the Sacraments. Neither is the effect of Christ's ordinance taken away by their wickedness, nor the grace of God's gifts diminished from such as by faith and rightly do receive the Sacraments ministered unto them; which be effectual, because of Christ's institution and promise, although they be ministered by evil men.

Nevertheless, it appertaineth to the discipline of the Church, that inquiry be made of evil Ministers, and that they be accused by those that have knowledge of their offences; and finally being found guilty, by just judgement be deposed.

XXVII. *Of Baptism.*
Baptism is not only a sign of profession, and mark of difference, whereby Christian men are discerned from others that be not christened, but it is also a sign of Regeneration or new Birth, whereby, as by an instrument, they that receive Baptism rightly are grafted into the Church; the promises of forgiveness of sin, and of our adoption to be sons of God by the Holy Ghost, are visibly signed and sealed; Faith is confirmed, and Grace increased by virtue of prayer unto God. The Baptism of

young Children is in any wise to be retained in the Church, as most agreeable with the institution of Christ.

XXVIII. *Of the Lord's Supper.*
The Supper of the Lord is not only a sign of the love that Christians ought to have among themselves one to another; but rather is a Sacrament of our Redemption by Christ's death: insomuch that to such as rightly, worthily, and with faith, receive the same, the Bread which we break is a partaking of the Body of Christ; and likewise the Cup of Blessing is a partaking of the Blood of Christ.

Transubstantiation (or the change of the substance of Bread and Wine) in the Supper of the Lord, cannot be proved by Holy Writ; but is repugnant to the plain words of Scripture, overthroweth the nature of a Sacrament, and hath given occasion to many superstitions. The Body of Christ is given, taken, and eaten, in the Supper, only after an heavenly and spiritual manner. And the mean whereby the Body of Christ is received and eaten in the Supper is Faith.

The Sacrament of the Lord's Supper was not by Christ's ordinance reserved, carried about, lifted up, or worshipped.

XXIX. *Of the Wicked which eat not the Body of Christ in the use of the Lord's Supper.*
The Wicked, and such as be void of a lively faith, although they do carnally and visibly press with their teeth (as Saint Augustine saith) the Sacrament of the Body and Blood of Christ, yet in no wise are they partakers of Christ: but rather, to their condemnation, do eat and drink the sign or Sacrament of so great a thing.

XXX. *Of both kinds.*
The Cup of the Lord is not to be denied to the Lay-people: for both the parts of the Lord's Sacrament, by Christ's ordinance and commandment, ought to be ministered to all Christian men alike.

XXXI. *Of the one Oblation of Christ finished upon the Cross.*
The offering of Christ once made is that perfect redemption, propitiation, and satisfaction, for all the sins of the whole world, both original and actual; and there is none other satisfaction for sin, but that alone. Wherefore the sacrifices of Masses, in the which it was commonly said, that the Priest did offer Christ for the quick and the dead, to have remission of pain or guilt, were blasphemous fables, and dangerous deceits.

XXXII. *Of the Marriage of Priests.*
Bishops, Priests, and Deacons, are not commanded by God's Law, either to vow the estate of single life, or to abstain from marriage: therefore it is lawful for them, as for all other Christian men, to marry at their own discretion, as they shall judge the same to serve better to godliness.

XXXIII. *Of excommunicate Persons, how they are to be avoided.*
That person which by open denunciation of the Church is rightly cut off from the unity of the Church, and excommunicated, ought to be taken of the whole multitude of the faithful, as an Heathen and Publican, until he be openly reconciled by penance, and received into the Church by a Judge that hath authority thereunto.

XXXIV. *Of the Traditions of the Church.*
It is not necessary that Traditions and Ceremonies be in all places one, and utterly like; for at all times they have been divers, and may be changed according to the diversities of countries, times, and men's manners, so that nothing be ordained against God's Word. Whosoever through his private judgement, willingly and purposely, doth openly break the traditions and ceremonies of the Church, which be not repugnant to the Word of God, and be ordained and approved by common authority, ought to be rebuked openly, (that others may fear to do the like,) as he that hath offendeth against the common order of the Church, and

hurteth the authority of the Magistrate, and woundeth the consciences of the weak brethren.

Every particular or national Church hath authority to ordain, change, and abolish, ceremonies or rites of the Church ordained only by man's authority, so that all things be done to edifying.

XXXV. *Of the Homilies.*

The second Book of Homilies, the several titles whereof we have joined under this Article, doth contain a godly and wholesome Doctrine, and necessary for these times, as doth the former Book of Homilies, which were set forth in the time of Edward the Sixth; and therefore we judge them to be read in Churches by the Ministers, diligently and distinctly, that they may be understood of the people.

Of the Names of the Homilies.

1. Of the right Use of the Church.
2. Against peril of Idolatry.
3. Of repairing and keeping clean of Churches.
4. Of good Words: first of Fasting.
5. Against Gluttony and Drunkenness.
6. Against Excess of Apparel.
7. Of Prayer.
8. Of the Place and Time of Prayer.
9. That Common Prayers and Sacraments ought to be ministered in a known tongue.
10. Of the reverend estimation of God's Word.
11. Of Alms-doing.
12. Of the Nativity of Christ.
13. Of the Passion of Christ.
14. Of the Resurrection of Christ.
15. Of the worthy receiving of the Sacrament of the Body and Blood of Christ.

16   Of the Gifts of the Holy Ghost.

17   For the Rogation Days.

18   Of the State of Matrimony.

19   Of Repentance.

20   Against Idleness.

21   Against Rebellion.

XXXVI. *Of Consecration of Bishops and Ministers.*
The Book of Consecration of Archbishops and Bishops, and Ordering of Priests and Deacons, lately set forth in the time of Edward the Sixth, and confirmed at the same time by authority of Parliament, doth contain all things necessary to such Consecration and Ordering: neither hath it any thing, that of itself is superstitious and ungodly. And therefore whosoever are consecrated and ordered according to the Rites of that Book, since the second year of the forenamed King Edward unto this time, or hereafter shall be consecrated or ordered according to the same Rites; we decree all such to be rightly, orderly, and lawfully consecrated and ordered.

XXXVII. *Of the Civil Magistrates.*
The King's Majesty hath the chief power in this Realm of England, and other his Dominions, unto whom the chief Government of all Estates of this Realm, whether they be Ecclesiastical or Civil, in all causes doth appertain, and is not, nor ought to be, subject to any foreign Jurisdiction.

Where we attribute to the King's Majesty the chief government, by which Titles we understand the minds of some slanderous folks to be offended; we give not to our Princes the ministering either of God's Word, or of the Sacraments, the which thing the Injunctions also lately set forth by Elizabeth our Queen do most plainly testify; but that only prerogative, which we see to have been given always to all godly Princes in Holy Scriptures by God himself; that is, that they should rule all estates and degrees committed to their charge by God, whether they be Ecclesiastical or Temporal, and restrain with the civil sword the stubborn and evildoers.

The Bishop of Rome hath no jurisdiction in this Realm of England.

The Laws of the Realm may punish Christian men with death, for heinous and grievous offences.

It is lawful for Christian men, at the commandment of the Magistrate, to bear weapons, and serve in the wars.

XXXVIII. *Of Christian men's Goods, which are not common.*
The Riches and Goods of Christians are not common, as touching the right, title, and possession of the same, as certain Anabaptists do falsely boast. Notwithstanding, every man ought, of such things as he possesseth, liberally to give alms to the poor, according to his ability.

XXXIX. *Of a Christian man's Oath.*
As we confess that vain and rash Swearing is forbidden Christian men by our Lord Jesus Christ, and James his Apostle, so we judge, that Christian Religion doth not prohibit, but that a man may swear when the Magistrate requireth, in a cause of faith and charity, so it be done according to the Prophet's teaching, in justice, judgement, and truth.

Appendix 5
The Canon Concerning Holy Orders 2004

The General Synod prescribes as follows:

Short title
1. This Canon may be cited as the "Canon concerning Holy Orders 2004".

Definitions
2. (1) In this Canon–
"authorising bishop", in relation to an ordination, means–
(a) the bishop of the diocese in which the ordination occurs; or
(b) if a bishop ordains a person for the bishop of another diocese, the bishop of that other diocese.
(2) Nothing in this Canon shall make it lawful for a woman to be ordained to the office of deacon in a diocese in which the Ordination of Women to the Office of Deacon Canon 1985 is not in force.
(3) Nothing in this Canon shall make it lawful for a woman to be ordained to
the office of priest or consecrated to the office of bishop in a diocese in which the Law of the Church of England Clarification Canon 1992 is not in force.

Bishops, priests and deacons
3. (1) A person shall not be accounted or taken to be a bishop, priest or deacon

in this Church unless, in accordance with this Canon or the law of this Church applying at the relevant time, the person–

(a) has been consecrated or ordained to that office by bishops, or a bishop, of this Church, or by bishops, or a bishop, of a Church in communion with this Church; or

(b) has been received into the ministry of this Church by a bishop of a diocese of this Church in accordance with the Holy Orders (Reception into Ministry) Canon 2004.

(2) A person shall not exercise the ministry of bishop, priest or deacon in this Church unless the person has been elected or appointed to an Episcopal office pursuant to the Constitution and ordinances of this Church and the ordinances of the relevant diocese and Province or is otherwise duly authorised as mentioned in section 14 to minister as a bishop, priest or deacon in this Church.

(3) A person does not have a right to be ordained deacon or priest or to be consecrated bishop.

Age

4. (1) Subject to sub-section (2)–

(a) a person shall not be ordained deacon unless the person is at least 23 years of age;

(b) a person shall not be ordained priest unless the person is at least 24 years of age.

(2) The Metropolitan of the Province in which the ordination of a deacon occurs or, where the ordination occurs in an extra-provincial diocese, the Primate, may, for reasons which seem to the Metropolitan or the Primate appropriate, dispense with the provisions of sub-section (1)(a).

Deacons

5. (1) A person shall not be ordained deacon unless on good and credible evidence the authorising bishop is satisfied that the person –

(a) has been baptised; and
(b) is a confirmed communicant member of this Church or has
(i) been received into this Church under the Reception Canon 1981 or any other law of this Church providing for the reception of persons into this Church; or
(ii) been received into a Church in communion with this Church under a law of that Church corresponding to the Reception Canon 1981 or a law of that Church providing for the reception of persons into that Church; and
(c) has a firm conviction of a calling by God to minister in Holy Orders as a deacon; and
(d) is of good character, as testified by a person specified by the authorising bishop; and
(e) is an active member of this Church or of a Church in communion with this Church and has been for no less than one year; and
(f) has completed appropriate training in theological and ministerial formation; and
(g) has a sufficient knowledge of Holy Scripture; and
(h) has a sufficient knowledge of and accepts the doctrine, discipline and principles of worship of this Church; and
(i) has a sufficient knowledge of the forms of worship of this Church; and
(j) has demonstrated the physical and mental capacity to minister.

(2) A person shall not be ordained deacon unless the authorising bishop is satisfied that the person has been designated to receive an appointment as a deacon in this Church in accordance with the Constitution and ordinances of this Church and the ordinances of the relevant diocese and Province.

(3) Notwithstanding sub-section (1) (e), a person–
(a) who has been ordained minister of another Christian Church; and
(b) of whom the authorising bishop is satisfied in respect of the other requirements of sub-section (1)–
may be ordained deacon.

Priests

6. (1) A person shall not be ordained priest unless on good and credible evidence the authorising bishop is satisfied that the person–
(a) is a deacon of this Church; and
(b) has ministered satisfactorily as a deacon for not less than 9 months or, for reasons satisfactory to the authorising bishop, for such shorter period as the authorising bishop approves; and
(c) has a firm conviction of a calling by God to minister in Holy Orders as a priest; and
(d) is of good character as testified by a person specified by the authorising bishop; and
(e) has completed appropriate training in theology and ministerial formation; and
(f) has a sufficient knowledge of Holy Scripture; and
(g) has a sufficient knowledge of, and accepts, the doctrine, discipline and principles of worship of this Church; and
(h) has a sufficient knowledge of the forms of worship of this Church; and
(i) has demonstrated the physical and mental capacity to minister.

(2) A person shall not be ordained priest unless the authorising bishop is satisfied that the person has been designated to receive an appointment as a priest in this Church in accordance with the Constitution and ordinances of this Church and the ordinances of the relevant diocese or Province.

Bishops

7. A person shall not be consecrated bishop unless on good and credible evidence the Metropolitan of the Province which includes the diocese for or in respect of which the consecration takes place or, in the case of an extra-provincial diocese, the Primate or, in either case, the diocesan bishop nominated by the Primate or the Metropolitan to act in the place of the Primate or the Metropolitan for such consecration pursuant to the Consecration of Bishops Canon 1966 is satisfied that the person–

(a) is of good character as testified by a person specified by the Metropolitan, Primate or other bishop as the case requires; and
(b) satisfies the requirements of canonical fitness; and
(c) has been duly elected or appointed to an Episcopal office in accordance with the Constitution and any other relevant canon or ordinance.

Ordaining bishop
8. Where an ordination under section 5 or 6 is not performed by the bishop of the diocese for which the person is being ordained, the ordaining bishop may act only on the written confirmation of the bishop of that diocese that the requirements of the relevant section have been satisfied.

Diaconate
9. Nothing requires that a deacon be at some time ordained priest, the office of deacon being recognised by this Church as a full and distinctive order within the historic ministry of this Church.

Ordinal or other form of service
10. A person shall be consecrated bishop or ordained priest or deacon in this Church in accordance with the Ordinal or a form of service authorised by General Synod.

Consecration
11. Sections 1 and 2 of the Consecration of Bishops Canon 1966 as in force immediately before the enactment of this Canon apply to and in respect of the consecration of a bishop.

Day and place of consecration
12. The consecration of a bishop shall take place upon some Sunday or Holy Day unless the Metropolitan or, in the case of an extra-provincial diocese, the Primate, for special reasons appoints some other day and shall take place

either in the metropolitical church of the Province or in a cathedral church or in another church or in some other place appointed by the Metropolitan or, in the case of an extra-provincial diocese, the Primate.

Place of ordination
13. Ordination to the office of priest or deacon shall take place either in the cathedral church of the diocese or in some other place nominated by the bishop.

Authority to minister
14. A bishop (not being the bishop of the diocese), a priest and a deacon may minister in that capacity in a diocese only after having received authority to do so from the bishop of the diocese, such authority ordinarily being given by licence under the hand and seal of the bishop or by written permission of the bishop.

Oaths etc and acceptance of codes of practice etc
15. (1) A bishop of a diocese, and an assistant bishop or a priest or deacon who has received authority from the bishop of a diocese to minister in that diocese shall take the oaths or affirmations, and make the declaration and assent, and the assent, required under the Oaths Affirmations Declarations and Assents Canon 1992 as adopted by the diocese or, if that Canon is not adopted by the diocese, such other oaths, affirmations, declarations and assents as are required under the law in force in that diocese.
(2) A bishop of a diocese, an assistant bishop or, a priest or deacon who has received authority from the bishop of a diocese to minister in that diocese shall declare acceptance of such codes of practice as are from time to time in force in the diocese.

Permission to officiate
16. The bishop of a diocese of this Church may permit a bishop, priest or

deacon consecrated or ordained in this Church or in a Church with which this Church is in communion, to officiate as a bishop, priest or deacon, as the case may be, in any parish or congregation of this Church within the diocese if the bishop has satisfactory evidence relating to the bishop's consecration or the priest or deacon's ordination and good standing.

Removal of bar to ordination
17. A person shall not be refused ordination as deacon or priest or consecration as a bishop on the ground that the person was born out of lawful wedlock.

Enforcement of Canon
18. (1) A person must not-
(a) in undertaking the whole, or any part, of any ordination or consecration (or purported ordination or consecration) in this Church; or
(b) in submitting or offering himself or herself for ordination or consecration in this Church,
knowingly act in contravention of this Canon.
(2) A person who breaches sub-section (1) will be taken to be in wilful violation of this Canon for the purposes of the Offences Canon 1962.

Canons 31 to 37
19. The Canons numbered 31 to 37, inclusive, of the Canons of 1603, insofar as the same may have any force, either in their original form or as amended or as affected by a law of this Church, shall have no operation or effect in a diocese of this Church which adopts this canon.

Coming into force by adoption
20. The provisions of this canon affect the order and good government of this Church within a diocese and shall not come into force in a diocese unless and until the diocese adopts this canon by ordinance of the synod of the diocese.

Appendix 6
The Oaths Affirmations Declarations and Assents Canon 1992

The General Synod prescribes as follows:

Short title

1. This canon may be cited as the "Oaths Affirmations Declarations and Assents Canon 1992"

Oath or Affirmation of Canonical Obedience

2. An oath or affirmation of canonical obedience shall be taken by a member of the clergy on
  (a) ordination to the diaconate,
  (b) ordination to the priesthood,
  (c) first licensing of the member by the bishop of a diocese
     (i) that member not having been ordained to the diaconate or priesthood in the diocese, or
     (ii) following service by that member outside the diocese pursuant to the licence of another bishop, and
  (d) consecration as an assistant bishop

Form of Oath or Affirmation of Canonical Obedience

3. (1) Whenever an oath of canonical obedience is taken by a member of the clergy or laity the following form shall be used -
"I .... do swear that I will pay true and canonical obedience

to .... [the bishop of the diocese or where applicable the bishop of the diocese sponsoring an ordination] and the successors of that bishop in all things lawful and honest. So help me God!"

(2) Whenever an affirmation of canonical obedience is taken by a member of the clergy or laity, the form in sub-section (1) shall be used but it shall be modified by –

(a) substituting for "swear" the phrase "solemnly and sincerely affirm"; and

(b) deleting the concluding sentence.

Declaration and Assent to Doctrine and Formularies

4. A declaration and assent to the doctrine and formularies of the Church shall be made by a member of the clergy on

(a) ordination to the diaconate,

(b) ordination to the priesthood,

(c) first licensing of the member by the bishop of a diocese
  (i) that member not having been ordained to the diaconate or priesthood in the diocese, or
  (ii) following service by that member outside the diocese pursuant to the licence of another bishop,

(d) consecration as an assistant bishop,

(e) consecration or installation as the bishop of a diocese,

and by a member of the laity on

(f) first licensing of that member by the bishop of a diocese.

Form of declaration and assent to doctrine and formularies

5. Whenever a declaration and assent to the doctrine and formularies of the Church is made by a member of the clergy the following form shall be used -

"I.................. firmly and sincerely believe the Catholic Faith and I give my assent to the doctrine of The Anglican Church of Australia as expressed in the Book of Common Prayer and the Ordering of Bishops, Priests and

Deacons and the Articles of Religion, as acknowledged in section 4 of the Constitution, and I believe that doctrine to be agreeable to the word of God. I declare my assent to the Fundamental Declarations of The Anglican Church of Australia as set out in sections 1, 2 and 3 of the Constitution.
In public prayer and administration of the sacraments I will use the form prescribed in the Book of Common Prayer or a form authorised by lawful authority and none other."

Assent to Constitutions and Laws

6. An assent to the constitutions and laws of the Church shall be required of a member of the clergy on
(a) ordination to the diaconate,
(b) ordination to the priesthood,
(c) first licensing of the member by the bishop of a diocese
   (i) that member not having been ordained to the diaconate or priesthood in the diocese, or
   (ii) following service by that member outside the diocese pursuant to the licence of another bishop,
(d) consecration as an assistant bishop,
(e) consecration or installation as the bishop of a diocese,
   and by a member of the laity on
(f) first licensing of that member by the bishop of the diocese.

Form of Assent to Constitutions and Laws

7. (1) Subject to sub-sections (2) and (3), whenever an assent to the constitutions and laws of the Church is made by a member of the clergy or the laity the following form shall be used -
"I .... do solemnly and sincerely declare my assent to be bound by the Constitution of the Anglican Church of Australia and the Constitution of the province of .... and of this diocese and by the canons, statutes, ordinances and rules, however described, from time to time of the synod of

this diocese and of the General Synod and the provincial synod (or council) which have force in this diocese."

(2) The form prescribed in sub-section (1) may be varied by deleting provincial references in a diocese which is not within a province.

(3) In a diocese in which a provision of the constitution of the diocese which is in force and which was in force on 1 January 1998 prescribes a different form of assent the diocesan form may be used instead of the form in subsection (1).

DIOCESAN PROVISION

8. (1) Nothing in this canon prevents the bishop or synod of a diocese requiring or providing for the use of any of the oaths, affirmations, declarations and assents referred to in this canon on occasions additional to those provided in this canon.

(2) Unless the bishop or synod of a diocese otherwise requires or provides, a person to be consecrated, ordained, instituted or licensed in this Church within the diocese is not required to take, make or subscribe to an oath, affirmation, declaration, assent or subscription not provided for or referred to in this canon.

Substantial Compliance

9. A deviation from the form of an oath, affirmation, declaration or assent prescribed in this canon which does not materially affect the substance shall be sufficient compliance with the requirements of this Canon.

Canon 36 of 1603 Repealed

10. Except to the extent that it requires a person to be licensed by the bishop of the diocese, the Canon numbered 36 of the Canons of 1603, insofar as it may have had any force either in its original form or as amended, shall have no operation or effect in a diocese which adopts this Canon.

Canon 7, 1973 Repealed

11. The Form of Declaration and Assent Canon 1973 is repealed.

Canon Affects Dioceses

12. The provisions of this canon affect the order and good government of this Church within a diocese and shall not come into force in a diocese unless and until the diocese adopts this Canon by ordinance.

Appendix 7
The Presentation, The Exhortation and Examination, and The Laying on of Hands from The Ordination of Deacons (APBA)

THE PRESENTATION

The archdeacon and a layperson, together with others if desired, present the ordinands to the bishop, saying N, bishop in the Church of God,
we present to you these persons/NN to be ordained deacon in the Church of God.

The bishop says

Can you assure us that they are suited by their learning and godly living to minister as deacons in the household of Christ, to the glory of God?

Those presenting the ordinands say

They have been examined.
Enquiries have been made among the people of God,
especially among those concerned with their preparation,
and we believe that these candidates are fit for this office.

The bishop says to the people

Dear friends in Christ, you know the importance of this office.
We have been assured that these persons are suited to this ministry.
If, however, any of you know an adequate reason why we should not proceed,
come forward and make it known.

THE EXHORTATION AND EXAMINATION

The bishop says to the candidate(s)
Our Lord and Saviour Jesus Christ lived and died
as the servant of God.
All who follow him are called to serve God in the world,
setting forward Christ's kingdom through the power of the Spirit.
Christ has called you to the office of deacon.
You are to be an ambassador of Christ,
serving God as you serve others in Jesus' name.
Proclaim the good news of God's love,
so that many may be moved to faith and repentance,
and hearts be opened to do justice,
love mercy, and walk humbly in the presence of God.
Let the transforming love of Jesus be known to all
among whom you live and work.
Strengthen the faithful, teach the young,
search out the careless and indifferent.
Encourage the members of Christ's body by word and example, ministering
among the sick, the needy and all who are oppressed or in trouble.
Together with your bishop, priest and people,
you are to take your place in public worship,
assist in the administration of the sacraments,
and play your part in the life and councils of the Church.
You are to preach the word of God in the place
to which you are licensed,
and to pray and work for peace and justice in the world.
As a deacon, you are to model your life according to the word of God.
Study the Scriptures, reflecting with God's people
upon their meaning,
that all may be equipped to live out God's truth in the world.
Put away all that does not make for holiness of life.

Be faithful in prayer, that you may have strength to run the race that is set before you.

And now, in order that this congregation may understand your intention, and so that your public profession may strengthen your resolve,

answer clearly these questions, which I ask you in the name of God and of the Church.

The bishop says

Do you believe that you are truly called to this order and ministry of deacons, being moved by the Holy Spirit to serve God and build up his people, according to the will of our Lord Jesus Christ and the order of this Anglican Church of Australia?

The ordinand(s) answer

I do believe I am called to this ministry.

Do you wholeheartedly accept the canonical Scriptures of the Old and New Testaments, as given by the Spirit to convey in many and varied ways the revelation of God which is fulfilled in our Lord Jesus Christ?

I do accept them.

Will you take your part in reading the holy Scriptures in the church and in assisting the priest to teach the doctrine of Christ and administer the sacraments?

I will, by God's grace.

Will you be diligent in prayer, and in the study of the holy Scriptures? Will you undertake such other studies as will help you in your ministry?

I will, by God's grace.

Will you strive to shape your own life, and that of your household, according to the way of Christ?

I will, by God's grace.

Will you constantly seek the help of the Holy Spirit to use and develop God's gifts to you, so that you may serve all by word and deed?

I will, by God's grace.

Will you promote unity, peace and love among all Christian people, especially among those with whom you serve God, encouraging and enabling them to fulfil their ministries?

I will, by God's grace.

Will you seek to set forward Christ's kingdom in the world, proclaiming the gospel and working for reconciliation, peace and justice?

I will, by God's grace.

Will you accept the order and discipline of the Anglican Church of Australia, submitting yourself to the lawful authority of your bishop and others set over you in the Church?

I will, by God's grace.

The bishop concludes

May God who has given you the will to do these things give you the grace and power to perform them. Amen.

The bishop says to the congregation

You have heard these persons respond to God's call.

Will you accept them as deacons in the Church of God?

The people reply

We accept them gladly!

Will you support and encourage them in this ministry?

We will, by God's grace.

A hymn invoking the Holy Spirit is sung.

THE LAYING ON OF HANDS

The candidate(s) kneel(s) before the bishop, who says

Blessed are you, Lord our God!
In your infinite love you set us free
to be a holy people in the kingdom of your Son.
Though he was rich, for our sake Christ became poor.
Taking the form of a servant, he humbled himself,
and gave his life a ransom for many.
Exalted as Lord of all,

he poured out the Spirit

and gave gifts to your people

to equip the saints for the work of ministry,

and to build up the body of Christ.

And now we give you thanks

that you have called these your servants

to the ministry of deacons in your Church.

Here the bishop lays hands on the head of each ordinand, and says

Send down the Holy Spirit upon your servant N,

whom we set apart by the laying on of our hands,

for the office and work of a deacon in your Church.

When hands have been laid upon all who are to be ordained deacon, the bishop continues

Grant to your servants, merciful God,

grace and power to proclaim the gospel of salvation.

May they be patient and loving, strong and steadfast.

As you have called them to your service,

make them worthy of their calling.

Accept our prayer through Jesus Christ our Lord,

who, with you and the Holy Spirit,

lives and reigns, one God, now and for ever.

The people respond

Amen.

Those on whom hands have been laid may be appropriately vested.

The bishop delivers to each a copy of the New Testament, saying

Take authority to exercise the office and ministry of a deacon in the Church of God, in the name of the Father, and of the Son, and of the Holy Spirit.

The people respond

Amen.

Appendix 8
The Presentation, The Exhortation and Examination, and The Laying on of Hands from The Ordination of Priests (APBA)

THE PRESENTATION

The archdeacon and a layperson, together with others if desired, present the ordinands to the bishop, saying

N, bishop in the Church of God,
we present to you these deacons/NN to be ordained priest.

The bishop says

Can you assure us that they are suited by their learning and godly living to minister as priests in the household of Christ?

Those presenting the ordinand(s) say

They have been examined.
Enquiries have been made among the people of God,
especially among those concerned with their preparation,
and we believe that these candidates are fit for this office.

The bishop says to the people

Dear friends in Christ, you know the importance of this office.
We have been assured that these deacons are suited to this ministry.
If, however, any of you know an adequate reason why we should not proceed,
come forward and make it known.

THE EXHORTATION AND EXAMINATION

The bishop says to the candidates

Our Lord Jesus Christ summons us all to obedience and discipleship.
In baptism we are called to be a royal priesthood,
a people belonging to God,
to make Christ known in all the world.
Now you are responding to the call of God and of the Church
to live and work as a priest, a pastor and teacher,
for God's glory and the strengthening of God's people.
You know the responsibility and significance of this office.
I now exhort you, in the name of Christ,
to take up your calling with joy and dedication.
As the Lord's messenger, proclaim the gospel of Jesus Christ.
Seek the lost, announce God's justice, warn and correct those in error.
You are to encourage and build up the body of Christ,
preaching the word of God,
leading God's people in prayer,
declaring God's forgiveness and blessing,
and faithfully ministering the sacraments of God's grace with reverence
and care.
Together with your bishop and other ministers,
you are to take your part in the life and councils of the Church.
Be a pastor after the pattern of Christ the great Shepherd, who laid down
his life for the sheep.
Be a teacher taught by the Lord in wisdom and holiness.
Lead the people of God as a servant of Christ.
Love and serve the people with whom you work,
caring alike for young and old, rich and poor, weak and strong.
Never forget how great a treasure is placed in your care:
the Church you must serve is Christ's spouse and body,
purchased at the cost of his own life.

Remember that you will be called to give account before Jesus Christ: if it should come about that the Church, or any of its members, is hurt or hindered as a result of your negligence, you know the greatness of the fault and the judgement that will follow. Therefore apply yourself with diligence and care, and fashion your life and ministry in accordance with Christ's example.
As you depend on the Holy Spirit and the grace of God,
put away all that does not make for holiness of life.
Clothe yourself with humility; be constant in prayer.
Study the Scriptures wholeheartedly,
reflecting with God's people upon their meaning,
so that your ministry and life may be shaped by Christ.
We have every confidence that you have already pondered these things deeply.
And now, in order that this congregation may understand your intention,
and so that your public profession may strengthen your resolve,
answer clearly these questions,
which we ask you in the name of God and of the Church.

The bishop says

Do you believe that you are truly called to this order and ministry of priests, according to the will of our Lord Jesus Christ and the order of this Anglican Church of Australia?

The ordinand(s) answer(s)

I believe I am called to this ministry.

Are you convinced that the holy Scriptures contain all doctrine necessary for eternal salvation through faith in Jesus Christ, and are you determined to instruct from these Scriptures the people committed to your care, teaching nothing as essential to salvation which cannot be demonstrated from the Scriptures?

I am convinced, and will do so by God's grace.

Will you be diligent in prayer, and in the study of the holy Scriptures?

I will, by God's grace.
Will you undertake such other studies as will help you in your ministry?
I will, by God's grace.
Will you constantly stir up the gift of God which is in you, so that you may proclaim the gospel of Christ?
I will, by God's grace.
Will you faithfully and humbly minister the doctrine, sacraments and discipline of Christ, as he has commanded and as this Church has received them?
I will, by God's grace.
Will you be ready, both in your public and private ministry, to oppose and set aside teaching that is contrary to God's word?
I will, by God's grace.
Will you be a faithful pastor to all whom you are called to serve and lead, striving together with them to build up the body of Christ in truth and love, in unity and peace?
I will, by God's grace.
Will you encourage and enable those committed to your care to fulfil their ministry and mission in the world?
I will, by God's grace.
Will you obey your bishop and other ministers given authority over you, gladly and willingly following their godly and lawful directions?
I will, by God's grace.

The bishop concludes

May God who has given you the will to do these things
give you the grace and power to perform them. Amen.

The bishop says to the congregation

You have heard these persons respond to God's call to love and serve him as priests.
Will you accept them as priests in the Church of God?

The people reply

We accept them gladly!
Will you support and encourage them in this ministry?
We will, by God's grace.
A hymn invoking the Holy Spirit is sung.

THE LAYING ON OF HANDS
The ordinand(s) kneel(s) before the bishop, who says
Blessed are you, Lord our God!
You have given us your only Son
to be the Apostle and High Priest of our faith,
and the Shepherd of our souls.
Exalted as Lord of all,
he poured out the Spirit and gave gifts to your people,
making some to be apostles, some prophets,
some evangelists, some pastors and teachers,
to equip the saints for the work of ministry,
and to build up the body of Christ.
And now we give you thanks
that you have called these your servants
to the ministry of priests in your Church.
Here the bishop with the priests present lay their hands on the head of each ordinand, and the bishop says
Send down the Holy Spirit upon your servant N,
whom we set apart by the laying on of our hands,
for the office and work of a priest in your Church.
When hands have been laid on all who are to be ordained priest, the bishop continues
Grant to these your servants, merciful God,
grace and power to fulfil their ministry:
to proclaim the gospel of salvation through word and sacrament,
to declare the forgiveness of sins,

and to watch over and care for the people committed to their charge.
As you have called them to your service,
make them worthy of their calling.
Accept our prayer through your Son, Jesus Christ our Lord,
to whom with you and the Holy Spirit belong glory and honour, worship
and praise, now and for ever.
The people respond
Amen.
Those on whom hands have been laid may be appropriately vested.
The bishop delivers to each a copy of the Holy Scriptures, saying
Take authority to preach the word of God, and to minister the holy sacraments in the congregation where you are appointed. Whose sins you forgive, they are forgiven; whose sins you retain, they are retained. Be a faithful minister of the word of God and of his holy sacraments.

Selected Resources

The Prayer Book

A Prayer Book for Australia 1995 © The Anglican Church of Australia Trust Corporation, 1995 (APBA)

The Book of Common Prayer and Administration of the Sacraments and other rites and ceremonies of the Church according to the use of The Church of England, 1662 (BCP)

Hefling, Charles. *The Book of Common Prayer: a guide.* Oxford University Press, 2021.

Sherlock, Charles. *Australian Anglicans worship: performing APBA.* Broughton, 2020.

Constitution and Canons

The Anglican Church of Australia, *Constitution*
https://anglican.org.au/governance/constitution/
The Anglican Church of Australia, *Canon and Rules*
https://anglican.org.au/governance/canons-and-rules/

Vocation and Call

Badcock, Gary. *The way of life: theology of vocation.* Grand Rapids: Eerdmans 1998.

Dewar, Francis. *Called or collared? An alternative approach to vocation.* London: SPCK, 2000.

Frame, Tom (Ed). *Called to minister: vocational discernment in the contemporary church.* Canberra: Barton, 2009.

Heywood, David. *Reimagining ministerial formation.* London: SCM, 2021.

Lawson, Johnathan & Gordon Mursell. *Hearing the call: stories of young vocation.* London: SPCK, 2014.

Thorp, Helen. *When the church says no.* Grove Books, 2004.

Ordained Ministry

Billings, Alan. *Making God possible: the task of ordained ministry present and future.* London: SPCK, 2010.

Cocksworth, Christopher & Rosalind Brown. *Being a priest today: exploring priestly identity.* Norwich: The Canterbury Press, 2006.

Cottrell, Stephen. *On priesthood: servants, shepherds, messengers, sentinels and stewards.* London: Hodder & Stoughton, 2020.

Friendship, John-Francis. *Enfolded in Christ: the inner life of a priest.* Norwich: The Canterbury Press, 2018.

Giles, Richard. *Here I am: reflections on the ordained life.* Norwich: The Canterbury Press, 2006.

Percy, Emma. *What clergy do: especially when it looks like nothing.* London: SPCK, 2014.

Pritchard, John. *The life and work of a priest.* London: SPCK, 2007.

Ramsay, Michael. *The Christian priest today.* London: SPCK, 1972.

Smith, Magdalen. *Steel angels: the personal qualities of a priest*. London: SPCK, 2014.

Tomlin, Graham. *The widening circle: priesthood as God's way of blessing the world*. London: SPCK, 2014.

Anglican Identity

Avis, Paul. *The Anglican understanding of the church: an introduction*. London: SPCK, 2nd edn, 2013.

Chapman, Mark. *Anglican Theology*. London: T&T Clark, 2012.

Chapman, Mark. *Anglicanism: A very short introduction*. Oxford University Press, 2006.

Davie, Martin. *Our inheritance of faith: A commentary on the thirty nine articles*. Gilead Books, 2013.

Giles, Richard. *How to be an Anglican: a beginner's guide to Anglican life and thought*. Norwich: The Canterbury Press, 2011.

Spencer, Stephen. *SCM study guide to Anglicanism*. London: SCM, 2010.

Throup, Marcus. *All things Anglican: who we are and what we believe*. Norwich: The Canterbury Press, 2018.

Wells, Samuel. *What Anglicans believe: an introduction*. Norwich: The Canterbury Press, 2011.

Anglicans in Australia

Davis, John. *Australian Anglicans and their Constitution*. Canberra: Acorn, 1993.

Deverell, Garry Worete. *Gondwana Theology: A Trawloolway man reflects on Christian Faith*. Morning Star, 2018.

Frame, Tom. *Anglicans in Australia*. Sydney: University of New South Wales Press, 2007.

Kaye, Bruce. *A church without walls: being Anglican in Australia*. Sydney: Dove, 1995.

Kaye, Bruce (Ed). *Anglicanism in Australia: a history*. Melbourne University Press, 2002.

www.ingramcontent.com/pod-product-compliance
Lightning Source LLC
Chambersburg PA
CBHW030300100526
44590CB00012B/457